Freedom

from

Stress

How To Take Control of Your Life

David Gamow
with Karen Gamow

Glenbridge Publishing Ltd.

Interior photos by George Beinhorn

Published by Glenbridge Publishing Ltd.
19923 E. Long Ave.
Centennial, Colorado 80016

Library of Congress Catalog Card Number: LC: 2006923775

International Standard Book Number: 978-0-944435-60-1

10 9 8 7 6 5 4 3 2 1

CONTENTS

PART I

This book is dedicated to

James D. Walters

Words are insufficient to express the gratitude I feel for his
friendship and wisdom, which made this book possible.

Also my deepest appreciation to my wife, Karen, whose
contributions were crucial to the completion of this book, and a true
life partner in more ways than I can count.

Part I

INTRODUCTION

S ome years ago we received a call from a woman who said she had taken the public version of our program a month earlier. She called us a bit later and said that attending was a last-ditch effort for her as she had been planning to commit suicide! She had taken the program in an attempt to turn her life around. In just the month that had passed since attending, she had faithfully practiced what she had learned and said she felt dramatically different. She then called us each Easter for the next few years to report on her progress. On her last call she told me she was going back to school to further herself, was in a new relationship, and felt a sense of control in her life that she had never experienced before. That was certainly an experience I will never forget and made me even more determined to share the power of these techniques as widely as possible. We have since received hundreds of notes of appreciation from people, though this woman's story is certainly the most dramatic.

This book is the result of a lifetime of study and personal practice as well as many years of lecturing and teaching. It is intended to be both practical and powerful.

Many books about stress talk about its causes and coping strategies, and though these are interesting topics, this book is different because it explores how to reduce your stress permanently and is not primarily an educational, academic, or "coping" tool.

I believe that what all people want is happiness, a sense of peace and freedom, and an enjoyment of life in its full range of experiences. But all too often our own fears, impulses, counterproductive desires, and emotions get in the way.

A good coach can bring the best out in someone who doesn't quite have the right knowledge or discipline to bring out the best by himself. Let this book be your personal coach so that all the different parts of you can work together to reach the goals you set in life. Your mental state can be eased, and the daily pushes and pulls can be brought to a fine point, much like twisting the end of a thread pulls the stray bits together before successfully guiding them through the eye of a needle. And rather than feeling pressured or defeated you will find an increased enjoyment of life.

A woman came to one of our corporate training programs a half-hour early. I pointed out to her that she was quite early, and she said that she had come, not to take the program, but to thank us because she had taken it six months earlier. She then started to cry and said her attendance at the program and subsequent practice of what she had learned had "changed everything." When we returned to that company six months later to do another program for a new group of employees, she came early once again to offer her thanks.

These practices have changed my life. I have great confidence that they can do the same for you, though each of us tends to manifest stress in a different way. When circumstances are especially difficult for someone to handle, he or she may become sad, depressed, withdrawn, or frightened. I have always been in the "hot reactor" camp. When something is not going my way, my stress tends to manifest itself as anger, annoyance, or irritation. I have spent more years than I prefer to count working on this unhelpful reaction (unhelpful to both the situation and to my own peace of mind), but since practicing what is covered in these pages, I have been able to move significantly *in the direction of* overcoming this tendency. Note my use of the phrase "in the direction of." It's not that I no longer am ever subject to such feelings. It is that there has been a steady improvement over time to a point where it is no longer a "problem." With patience and steady effort it can be done. If I can do it, so can you.

The mind operates according to a set of laws, just as the body operates according to the laws, of nutrition, health, physics, and chemistry. When we cooperate with those laws, we feel harmony and at peace with the world around us. When we live a life in conflict with those laws, we always feel as though we are swimming upstream, which over extended periods of time is exhausting and results in stress and constant feelings of conflict and pressure. These laws are impersonal. They are not out to get us, nor are they someone's creation. When we touch a hot stove we get burned. We can complain about it, wonder why it has to be so, even pretend it is not true, but the result is always the same.

Pain is the body's way of telling us to change our behavior. If, for example, we keep eating the wrong foods and take various medications to cover up the problems that result, we are missing the body's message that a change in our eating pattern is what's needed. Treating the symptom does not generally accomplish much, except to put off the day of reckoning. In exactly the same way, *if we are feeling significant stress in our lives and are not taking it as an indication that we have something that needs changing, we are ignoring important information that is being provided.* Prolonged periods of stress and repeated difficult emotional reactions to what life presents to us are not resolved through drinking, shopping, or watching TV. These diversions are sometimes used to cover up the symptoms by dulling or diverting attention from the pain. Our discomfort is a sign that something needs to change.

But we cannot know what to change unless we understand the mechanism that is causing the discomfort. If we never come to understand that it was the hot stove that caused the burn, we might feel the pain but not realize what to do to avoid it. This book will make clear, not only what is causing our stress, but how to change what needs to be changed.

The kind of changes we are talking about require neither Herculean effort nor giving up important aspects of your life. They only require a moderate level of discipline and a sincere effort to change in order to become free from stress.

Many times after a program, one or several people will approach me and ask whether there is a book that captures what they have just experienced. I can now answer that question in the affirmative. I hope it starts you on your way to a significantly happier, healthier, and more dynamic and effective future.

Please read and reread the pages that follow. Read them slowly. Much of what is presented may seem simple at first but upon deeper thought requires a dramatic change of perspective. Don't skim over a section and think, "Yeah. That makes sense. I get it," unless you really feel the truth of what is being said along with its many implications. Don't approach what you read as if it were "information." Please don't just "observe" what is presented here as if strolling casually through a museum. This approach is for *you*, personally, and I know, after experiencing its power with many thousands of people, that it holds keys to resolving the kinds of long-standing difficulties that over time defeat us in a profound sense. Approach these pages as you would a doctor whom you believe can cure or improve a condition that has been plaguing you for years: approach these pages with hope, with enthusiasm, with great energy, and with concentration. May these ideas help you, as they have helped me and so many others, to move towards a life filled with the happiness and joy that we all seek.

I

WHAT IS STRESS?

This book deals primarily with what is happening inside our minds when we find ourselves under stress. Stress is a mental phenomenon, and it is there where the real battle needs to be fought. Yet it seems appropriate to look at the physical component first, because that is its ancient root and because it is there where the symptoms are most likely to first be noticed.

We are preprogrammed to respond to challenging situations in a way that has historically served us, but is less helpful in modern society. When we are in the presence of a perceived threat, our body automatically kicks into high gear. The hypothalamus (a part of the brain near its center) secretes a chemical called CRH. This chemical in turn activates the pituitary gland, which is located at the base of the brain. The pituitary gland secretes a chemical called ACTH, which in turn stimulates the adrenal glands near the base of the lungs. The adrenals release cortisol, a hormone that keeps our energy high by keeping our blood sugar up. The adrenals also produce epinephrine that increases our heart rate and breathing rate. The legs and arms also receive extra blood for the added energy to face whatever is coming. When we feel a rush of energy in a threatening situation, it is this chain of events that gives us that boost in order to meet the challenge. A very complex set of automatic reactions and all in all a pretty good system, except. . . .

We are rarely faced with sudden external challenges these days, and thus this mechanism is not as useful. When was the last time you were attacked by a wild boar? When something large has fallen over in our house, or we are running to catch the bus, the standard chain of events described above works pretty well. But what good are those extra chemicals that are preparing us for battle when we're at work sitting next to an annoying co-worker who hums loudly all day long? What do we do when we're stuck for an hour in traffic almost every day, with tailgaters, "line-cutters," and the entire menagerie we face every day on the roads? The extra blood in our arms and legs is not very useful when our computer crashes!

Our biomechanical programming is set up to respond to short-term immediate physical threats. Low-level threats that continue over long periods of time burn us out and "use us up" until our nervous system is frayed from the constant "red alerts," and our various body systems start to break down. Neuroscientists have estimated that primitive man would have a stress response two to three times a day. That is, his body would initiate the biochemical changes we have described the few times a day a threat occurred. It is estimated that modern man has this stress response activated 30–50 times a day! After years of chronic over-activation we begin to experience the host of things medicine now knows are stress related: high blood pressure, insomnia, aches and pains, headaches, inability to focus the mind, feelings of helplessness, immune system weaknesses, and unfortunately much more. Scientists also keep discovering additional negative results from this constant state of stress. But the good news is they have also learned that we can do something about it. You are about to unlock the secrets to turning off, or at least dramatically slowing down, this process.

Definition of Stress

The word *stress* is common, but we must be clear as to what we mean in the way we will be using it. We want a definition that focuses more on attitude and perception than on the physical characteristics we have thus far discussed. We are trying to get at the root cause of stress and not just describe the physiological changes that happen. We cannot directly access the adrenal glands or hypothalamus and turn them off. Knowing what is happening physically is interesting, but may not help us to change what we need to change. The source of the stress is perceptual and therefore based in the mind.

The definition most useful for our purposes is: *Stress is created by the gap between how the world is and how we want it to be.* Who among us has the world exactly as he would like it to be? No one. Neither us nor anyone we know. This is why everyone feels some degree of stress. Everyone has a gap between how the world is and how he or she wants it to be.

Picture your two index fingers held up in front of your eyes. The world's changes can be shown by your right hand moving farther to the right. This movement of the finger (world) increases the gap between the two fingers and therefore indicates more stress. When we desire to close the gap, we naturally spend all of our energy trying to get the right finger to move back closer to the left in order to reduce the gap and thereby reduce stress. This seems to make perfect sense.

But there is a second option: move the left hand towards the right hand instead. The right hand is our circumstances, but the left hand is us. Instead of closing the gap by changing our circumstances, we can reduce the gap by changing ourselves. Both movements narrow the gap and result in decreased stress.

This book is about *freedom*, the freedom to consciously choose when to move the right hand (change our circumstances) and when to move the left hand (change ourselves). If we could master the ability to change the location of *either* our left finger (ourselves) or our right finger (our circumstances) our stress would drop to virtually zero, we would become enormously happier and more satisfied with life, and we would become incredibly effective at whatever we put our minds to. The problem is that when we are feeling stress, we *always* think the only solution is to move the right hand (change our circumstances). We shall now explore the two ways we seek to rectify this situation.

Two Approaches to Conquering Stress

Everyone faces difficulties every day, from enormous to trivial. But we have all observed humanity's tremendous range of responses to those difficulties. Some people embrace them, others seek to run from them. Some accept them dynamically while others reject and deny them. Some put out more energy to meet the challenges while still others give up and sink under their weight. Some become angry or annoyed with the circumstances while others simply beat themselves up. We may not always be able to change our circumstances into ones of our liking but we can, and must, embrace and improve what happens *inside us* when we are faced with them.

We can dramatically change the level of stress in our lives by learning how to work with both our minds' perceptions and the physiological effect those perceptions have on the brain. Working with both the physical brain and the cognitive mind is quite effective as each approach complements and reinforces the other. This is much more effective than either approach taken on its own. The first part of the book will examine the perceptions and attitudes we hold that create our stress. Later, we will examine what we can do to halt stress on the physiological level, offering specific meditation and breathing techniques that have been clinically tested and proven to reverse the harmful biochemical events described earlier.

Stress Is Not in Circumstances

We tend to think that stress is a function of our circumstances. Let's suppose you are on the highway on your way to a formal function. You're in your best clothes and running a bit late. Suddenly one of your tires goes flat. We might describe such an event as a "tough spot" or "a tense circumstance," but these words and phrases are misleading. After all, the *situation* is not tense. The tire is not tense. The highway is not stressed. You're tense! The descriptions we tend to use describe the external situation and not what is happening inside of *us*. Stress is a function of how we respond to situations and is not somehow "in" the situation itself. A simple example will make this clear.

How a Change of Perspective Affects Stress

Suppose you're standing on a bus and someone bumps into you from behind with a sharp elbow in the ribs. You're annoyed and turn around to see who did it and see that the person who bumped you is blind. What happens? Almost certainly you're instantly less annoyed. If anything, you feel compassion for him rather than continuing to think about yourself and your hurt ribs. This is a very instructive example for a number of reasons:

a) Notice that the physical reality didn't change. Your ribs hurt exactly as much as they did before you turned around. Circumstances, in this case hurt ribs, do not cause stress.

b) Notice also that you didn't repress your feelings. It took no act of will to remove your annoyance. Nor were you restraining yourself by thinking, "My mother always told me not to yell at blind people!"

c) You didn't take six months to get over your anger by processing it with a therapist or with friends. You also didn't just wait for the difficult feelings to pass on their own. The change was immediate once your perception changed.

d) And finally, you didn't practice any "tips" or quick fixes. What I mean by tips is the long list of things people do to temporarily reduce their stress: exercise, pet your dog, listen to soothing music, take a bath, drink herbal tea, etc. It's not that these things are not comforting, but they do not change things in any lasting or deep way.

Where, then, did the annoyance go? By what mechanism was it made to disappear? Your stress went away for the simple reason that your *perception* changed. You simply saw something that you hadn't previously seen, and with that new perception the stress simply vanished, even if the physical pain did not.

What would have happened if you had gotten off that bus without turning around? You could potentially have been annoyed for some time as you recounted the episode to friends. All because you didn't take the time to turn around. What if you had turned around but had not been able to tell he was blind? You still would have been annoyed. I made it easy for you by telling you that he couldn't see. If you had gotten off before looking or hadn't noticed his affliction, you'd have been annoyed simply because there was something you didn't know. Well, there is always something we don't know! One of our strategies will be to learn how to remove the blinders from our eyes and see what we had not previously seen. This will dramatically change our perceptions, which will in turn dramatically lower our stress.

In the infinite variety of situations we face in life, each change of perception awakens in us a new feeling of compassion, sorrow, joy, anger, regret, or a host of other either pleasant or unpleasant feelings and emotions. We think stress is somehow inherent in the event or situation, but it is the *perception* of the event or situation that is the true cause. This is good news. While we may not be able to change our circumstances, we can change our perceptions because, after all, they are within us. We don't need other people to cooperate with us to succeed. This ability opens the door for us to work with ourselves in a way that is both profound and remarkably effective.

Unfortunately, all humans seem to be preprogrammed with a few basic *mis*perceptions. These chronic misperceptions have an unfortunate result. They act as a fertilizer that makes the soil of our minds rich and fertile for the slightest seed of stress, which is then able to sprout into a nice healthy "stress plant."

We're going to explore what those misperceptions are and how we can change them. This process will make our mental soil much less hospitable to stress, so that when circumstances arise that used to bother us, the seeds will simply land on barren soil and fail to take root and grow. We will have taken a giant step in making ourselves immune to stress.

A wonderful side benefit of this approach is that we will be able to remain engaged with difficult situations, rather than fleeing from them (mentally or literally) to avoid the stress we had associated with them. This will enable us to address and solve previously insurmountable long-standing problems where we used to have a stress-filled response.

The stress response itself often inhibits our solving the problem that we believe caused our stress in the first place. When we are experiencing stress, we simply do not think clearly. It's as if someone said to us, "Relax, or I'll really let you have it!" When we most need to relax, our own desires and reactions create the stress that inhibits our very efforts to relax.

Notice, too, that this approach does not use any of the stress-reducing tips referred to before, such as working out, listening to nice music, or spending time with good friends. It is true that after exercise, your level of stress is reduced, but this is of short-term benefit only. Imagine having a bad day, getting home, going for a run to work off the day's tensions, and then feeling better. The next day, however, you have another bad day, so you run and feel better again. This is similar to cutting the heads off the dandelions in your lawn. Your lawn looks great for a while, but then all the heads come back just as bright, yellow, and intrusive as ever. Nothing has really changed other than your temporary head-cutting fix has worn off. Of course we all know that it is far better to get weeds out by the roots, for that's the only way to get lasting results.

Barnacles plague ships. They grow on the sides and use a strong natural cement to make sure they stay there. You might spend quite a bit of time trying to figure out ways to remove those barnacles. But far better would be to figure out how to build ships that barnacles cannot stick to! I don't recommend coming up with new and improved tricks for working off each day's accumulation of stress. A far better strategy would be to turn yourself into the kind of person that doesn't allow stress to stick in the first place. Make yourself barnacle-proof. Now you've really got something!

We have seen in the story of the bus episode that the stress was dependent on perception, not on the physical reality of the hurt ribs. While this example is of a minor situation, the same perceptual mechanism is at work in even our most difficult challenges. For now, we will discuss only more minor difficulties, as this is the best way to see the physics of what is happening. Later on, armed with the insights we have gained through starting small, we will show how *all* difficulties follow the same path.

II

HOW TO ACHIEVE CLARITY
OF MIND

W hy is it that you always give good advice to your friends? You can always tell what they should do and often give them advice that is right on the mark. You do not, however, have the same insight with the situations you yourself face.

Why is it that during a difficult interaction with someone you often don't know what to say? But three hours later you think, "Now I know what I should have said!" Why does the insight come three hours later? It's not as if you went to the library for the three hours and researched the question!

Why is it that it is so easy to see everyone else's flaws, but not your own? It's not, unfortunately, because your flaws are so miniscule since so many others can see them.

All three of these situations can be explained by a single idea: *When we are personally and emotionally involved with what is happening to us, we lose our clarity.*

Some years ago, my wife and teaching partner, Karen, was in a complicated situation. She said to me, "I just can't

18

figure out what to do." When we can't figure out what to do in a situation, it is almost never because we don't have enough information, nor is it because we are not intelligent enough. Our uncertainty and confusion is a result of being *personally and emotionally involved* with whatever situation is puzzling us. In that state we simply don't see clearly. Stepping back and becoming an observer instead of an emotionally involved participant, results in clarity.

With this in mind, I said to her, "Come over here for a minute." She walked over and stood next to me with both of us facing a blank wall. I then said, "Pretend that you're watching a movie on that wall. The heroine of the movie is in the following situation . . ." and I then described the situation Karen had been unable to figure out. I made it very clear that the woman in the movie was not her, but someone else. It took a few minutes for her to change her orientation, so she could really feel the setup I had described.

After I felt she was fully engaged in "watching the movie," I asked her what advice she would give the heroine. She immediately had two very good suggestions. Turning back to look at her instead of the wall, I said, "Well, why don't those ideas work for you, since you're in the same situation as the woman in the movie?" She immediately realized that her proposed solutions did work for her, solutions that she had not previously seen. She had come up with the solutions herself, whereas before watching the movie she was completely stumped.

Why does this trick work? Because once we step back and look at the movie we're no longer personally and emotionally involved. This is why we are able to give good advice to our friends: because they are not us! When it's someone else, we're not personally and emotionally involved and we can just be an observer. Stepping back to watch the movie is also why we know what to say three hours later. Think about what we tend to do three hours later. We are reviewing what happened in our mind's eye, mentally replaying the scene as it had unfolded. We picture what happened and think, "Well, I said this, and he said that, so why didn't I just say such and such?" What are we doing? We're looking back at the scene as if it were a movie or a play, in the same way Karen did in the previous story.

But why wait three hours to do this? Our emotional involvement becomes less and less over time in a natural way because, as it is said, "time heals all wounds." As the emotion recedes, we become calmer and clearer. But what if there were a way to accelerate this natural process? Why would we choose to wait three hours to get clarity? Why not two hours? Why not ten minutes? Why wait any time at all? We can train ourselves to lessen our personal and emotional involvement immediately rather than waiting for it to diminish gradually over time. This is what martial artists and emergency service personnel are trained to do. They mentally step back and "watch the movie" as soon as the situation demands it. Let's see what this looks like in the middle of a real-life difficult circumstance.

In the Heat of Battle

Karen and I were on the highway when she changed lanes and pulled in front of someone who felt we had pulled in front of him too closely. You know what that's like. I looked over and he seemed to have smoke pouring out of his ears. He was clearly agitated and was waving both arms at us. (I must say, it's a little scary driving next to someone who is waving both arms at you!) He was also shouting something that I fortunately couldn't hear. But as I looked over, I thought, "Wow! A movie of a crazy person in a car. Gosh, I never even knew faces could turn that color. Hey, Karen, look at that guy in the car next to us; isn't he interesting looking? And look at that vein in his forehead – I bet it's going to blow!" There was no stress there as I was just an observer watching the movie. There was no need to become personally and emotionally involved with his antics. Watching a movie of a crazy person in a car does not need to become a stressful event for the movie viewer. That his ranting was directed at us doesn't change anything nor does it force us to have any particular set of feelings in response.

It may seem as if what I am suggesting is to not care about other people. If you don't care about anyone or anything, you'd certainly feel less stress. But there is more to the story. Watching the movie works to reduce our personal and emotional involvement and thus our stress, but when done properly, it also enables us to stay fully engaged and caring at the same time.

Little Children Yell to Warn the Movie Hero

Have you ever been to the movies with a group of small children? Let's say it's a Western. Cowboy Bob is riding down the trail minding his own business, but there's a bad guy crouched behind a rock who is going to ambush Cowboy Bob. What are all the little kids doing? They're all yelling at the movie, "Look out, Cowboy Bob!

He's behind the rock!" And we're in the audience laughing because it's so cute. The children seem not to understand that yelling at the movie is not helpful and won't change anything.

But how is this different than what we do? When your computer freezes in the middle of an important project, how do you respond? If you're like most people, your first thought is something like, "You stupid computer!" This is simply the adult version of yelling at Cowboy Bob. Our yelling at our computer is no more sensible than what we were laughing at the children for doing.

When you're late for an appointment, take the ramp onto the highway, and see a sea of red taillights, isn't your first thought, "Oh my gosh! Where did all these cars come from?!" The other drivers, of course, will soon be looking at you thinking the same thing.

Each of us "yells at the movie" many times a day. We do this because we want the world to be different. And we want the world to be different because we're convinced that unless the world behaves the way we want it to, we can never be happy. We wish the laws of physics could be temporarily suspended, but wishing somehow doesn't make it so. When physics (or some other person!) is being stubborn, what we *can* do is move the finger that represents us rather than wishing things were different or complaining about the world the way it is.

A Quick Cure For a Long-Term Problem

A woman had been on an endless cycle of visits to chiropractors, osteopaths, and doctors for chronic neck pain that had been troubling her for thirteen years. She would get a treatment and feel better – for an hour, a half day, or sometimes a bit more. But after a short time her pain would be back, just as severe as before the treatment. The root of the problem was not being addressed, as the deeper source was that her situation at work was making her so tense that her neck was being pulled out of alignment. Putting it back was a temporary fix at best because the next day she was back in her stressful job and her neck would go out again. She attended our program in hopes that what we taught would make a difference.

We saw her again about two weeks later when we returned for a follow-up program at the same company. She told us that in just the two weeks since she started practicing what she had learned, her chronic neck pain had all but disappeared. As we teach a number of techniques relating to pain management, I asked her what specifically seemed to make this happen. Her answer surprised me. She said "watching the movie" had changed everything for her. She related the following story:

> I work in the copier room of a large corporation. It's very stressful. People come in all day long with rush jobs, under crushing deadlines. To make things worse, making the copies is always the very last thing people do, so virtually everyone who comes to see me is already late! Their stress was unfortunately easily transmitted to me. I would rush around getting their work done and feel a moment of relief when I got it to them. But then the next person would come in and the cycle would start again. By the end of each day my neck was a wreck.
>
> But using the movie technique has changed everything. Someone recently came to my work space and

> aggressively demanded, "Where's my job?!" I mentally
> took a step back and watched a movie of a person
> saying, "where's my job?" so I answered him calmly,
>> "It's not ready yet."
>> "Why isn't it ready?"
>> "The machine is broken."
>> "When is it going to be fixed?"
>> "Tomorrow afternoon."
> I was able to stay calm the whole time he aggres-
> sively cross-examined me.

What was she seeing in the "movie?" A man in a copy
center who was frustrated because he couldn't get his
work done. Her straightforward and calm answers were
possible because she wasn't personally and emotionally
involved and was just the observer.

Unfortunately, what might a more typical interaction
sound like?

> "Where's my job?"
> "It's not ready yet."
> "Why not?!"
> "The darn machine is broken."
> "Well, fix it!"
> "It's not my job to fix it."
> "What do you mean it's not your job to fix it? You
> work here, don't you?"
> "Yeah, but I'm not responsible for machine mainte-
> nance."
> "Well, who's responsible for machine mainte-
> nance?"
> "Oh, that's George and he's out this week."
> "What do you mean he's out this week?!"
> "Don't yell at me. I already told you – I do docu-
> ment production, not scheduling!"

And so on with each party getting more and more agitated and upset with each succeeding go-round. What she actually reported to me was that after mentally stepping back and watching the scene unfold, she would have this exchange instead:

> "By the way, did you know there's a copy machine in the building next door?"
> "There is?"
> "Yes. I can't go and do it for you, but it has an auto-feed. It'll take you only about ten minutes."

She told him where it was, and he left, quite happy to get his job done. She was also happy as well. (Of course – he was gone!) The job got done and the company was served. What did it cost? Nothing. How long did it take? No time at all. All from stepping back and watching the movie rather than becoming personally and emotionally involved.

When Do We Help Others?

It could be that it was easy for her to step back mentally because she didn't care about him or his work. While lack of caring may help avoid becoming personally and emotionally involved, such an attitude is definitely not what is being suggested here.

Suppose you're walking down the street and you see a man trying to move a box. It's very light as it only has a thin plastic tube in it, but it's sixteen feet long, and at that length it's too awkward to carry, so he's holding one end and dragging it down the sidewalk. He also happens to be going the same direction as you. You know the box is light, you're in no hurry, and he's only going one more block. You'd most likely offer to help. Why not? So you cheerfully say, "Let me give you a hand" and take the other end. You get where he was going and drop the box off. He's very appreciative, and you feel good for having helped out.

Suppose now we imagine an identical situation: same man, same box, same you. Everything is identical except for two things: The first is that you know that he's quite angry and in a foul mood. The second is that you know his anger is with you because he thinks it's your fault that he has to move that darn box! Now what are you likely to do? If you're like most people, you'd cross the street, walk the other way, glance at your watch as if you had to be somewhere else, or just avoid him in some other way. What changed? The box is not heavier. You're not a less helpful person. The only thing that changed was that as soon as you knew he was blaming you, you suddenly became personally and emotionally involved. When you're personally and emotionally involved with something, your top priority is to protect yourself. The last thing you're interested in or thinking about is helping him (or anyone else).

When we're personally and emotionally involved, we become much less oriented towards helping others. Even the thought that he *might* blame you tends to create instant personal and emotional involvement. Once that happens, your goals and desires immediately change. You're not a less kind person than you were nor a less helpful one. It is just that once your perspective and goals change, your behavior follows your new set of attitudes.

Once you're thinking about yourself and not him, everything changes.

When you were *not* personally and emotionally involved, your natural inclination was to help. As soon as you saw him struggling, your first thought was, "Let me give you a hand." Staying the observer inclines us to help more and does not encourage an uncaring attitude. Being personally and emotionally involved promotes caring, but not of anything other than ourselves!

When the woman in the copy center took a step back to look at the "movie," she was simply watching a movie of a co-worker who was frustrated that he couldn't get his work done. Her mind immediately moved toward helping him. Why not? If you would help a stranger on the street with a box, why wouldn't you help a co-worker? Why wouldn't you help someone you love and care about – someone in your own family? There's only one answer: because when we become personally and emotionally involved, we are thinking more about us than them. The trick is to avoid becoming personally and emotionally involved when someone is blaming us. In fact, as we will see, it is best not to become personally and emotionally involved in any situation.

Sometimes people think this is a recipe for becoming wooden, uninvolved, and unfeeling. It most definitely is not. We will explore this in detail a bit later and see that this approach actually enables us to become more caring, more compassionate, more alive, and more feeling. But for now we must still develop our present idea further.

The solutions posed above (helping with the box and suggesting the copy machine next door) are simple and helpful. Yet we often engage in counterproductive behavior instead. We've undoubtedly been getting this wrong for many years. How many times have we "defended" ourselves from a perceived slight or attack and actually made things worse? Clearly there must be some sort of short circuit in our brains to engage in useless, counterproductive behavior time after time over many years. If this is so, the obvious question is: what is the nature of the short circuit? And more importantly, how do we repair it?

III

WHY WE FEEL STRESS

Think about how many people you know. Let's assume that it's about a hundred. Let's assume further that they average forty years in age. The total life experience of all of those people added together comes to 4,000 years. How many seconds are there in 4,000 years? Over one hundred billion – quite a large number. Here's a remarkable thing to think about: Not for one single second in that 4,000 year span of time has even one of those people had every single circumstance in their lives line up just as they would like. We think that if we could only get everything lined up the way we want it, we could finally relax and be happy. Since this state of affairs has never occurred for you or anyone you know for even one second, getting everything the way you want it to be doesn't seem like much of a strategy for finding peace or happiness!

If only we had the right job, enough money, the right relationship, the right body weight and appearance, the right friends, a better car, a better home, more free time, better health . . . the list goes on forever.

There's an interesting story of a man who always wanted a sports car. One day it was his great good fortune to find a lamp labeled "Magic Lamp." Having read many childhood stories he immediately knew what to do and gave the lamp a good rub. Of course, out popped a genie. But this genie was different and granted twenty wishes! The man immediately asked for the sports car he had always wanted. It instantly appeared in front of him.

He was very happy but after a time realized that he should have gotten a red one instead of the blue one the genie had manifested. He thus asked for a color change and the car was immediately made a beautiful bright red. Soon, however, it had some engine trouble, and he learned that parts for such an exotic car were quite expensive. No problem, with eighteen wishes left he soon had a car with an engine that would last forever and never break down. But his joy was short-lived as a parking lot accident damaged his new toy. A wish fixed the car and gave it an indestructible body at the same time. Knowing that it could not be damaged, however, resulted in quite a number of speeding tickets, but with fifteen wishes left he soon had his tickets erased. One more wish saw to it that he would not be ticketed again. But unfortunately he had forgotten about . . . .

Even with so simple a thing as a car there is almost an infinite number of things that can go wrong. When looking at the entire spectrum of life, the number of possible snafus is truly endless. Depending on everything to go our way for us to be happy and satisfied is the height of folly and gets worse. Even if by some miracle you managed to get everything lined up perfectly, you would instantly become nervous that something might change.

If Our Mind Is Not Our Friend, Nowhere Is Safe

A friend of mine likes to share this image that illustrates this point well: Imagine that you are lying on the beach. It's a perfect day and you're thoroughly enjoying yourself. You've been saving for two years for this Caribbean vacation and have sprung for a gorgeous four-star hotel. Everything seems perfect, and you have three whole weeks! As you're lying there, however, it occurs to you how great it would be to take photos. Unfortunately, your camera got lost a few weeks before the trip. You wanted to get a new one soon, but, having spent as much as you did on the vacation, were hesitant to do so. Of course, you think, if they paid you what you deserved at work, this wouldn't be a problem! They've been talking about giving you a raise for over a year, and it still hasn't happened. Suddenly you notice you're in quite a little mood about your mistreatment at work. You had been feeling great a few minutes ago but now . . . .

What happened? Our vacationer was having a wonderful trip – one she had been looking forward to for years – but now her whole trip was ruined as she became consumed with thoughts about her pay at work. What changed? Absolutely nothing – only her own thoughts and attitudes.

You could be on the finest beach in the finest paradise on Earth and be just as unhappy as you were when you were back home. Stress, unhappiness, dissatisfaction – these things are not inherent in circumstances and cannot be cured even by the finest beach. They are born and nurtured in us. Research has shown that lottery winners who have finally won the money they have always wanted wind up being no more happy than they were before.

> Sure, if a person is handed $10, the pleasure centers of his brain light up as if he were given food, sex, or drugs. But that initial rush does not translate into long-term pleasure for most people. Surveys have found virtually the same level of happiness between the very rich individuals on the Forbes 400 and the Masai herdsmen of East Africa. Lottery winners return to their previous level of happiness after five years.*

A study reported by the University of California regents compared the happiness of lottery winners and individuals that sustained a physical injury. What they found was that though there were changes in the expected direction for each group, they quickly returned to their pre-event level of happiness, the winners losing their happiness and the injured people regaining theirs. This research suggests that we adapt to these situations very quickly, and that the circumstances only have a brief effect.

That level of happiness to which we return can be thought of as our natural emotional balance point. We can move off that point for a time, but the real goal ought to be moving the point itself. It's through the practices that we develop here that our natural balance point can be moved. And moving it changes us in fundamental and important ways. Adding some external detail to our lives may move us off that point for the better for a time, but such an advantage is fleeting. We then look for the next short-term fix to move us off that point again, but it too

---

*Mathew Harper, "It's Official: Money Can't Buy Happiness," *Forbes*, 9/23/04.

lasts only a short time. The only lasting help comes from moving the point itself independent of short-term external boosts. Developing a habit of stepping back and looking at the "movie" changes our very relationship to the world around us, which in turn determines the actual location of our emotional balance point.

The habit of becoming personally and emotionally involved also prevents us from knowing what to do about any difficulties we may face. Whenever you *can't* tell what to do in a given situation, you can be sure that it's because you are personally and emotionally involved. As soon as you step back, you will clearly see what is happening and know what to do (if anything).

How to Make Good Choices

Being the observer enables us to see clearly and to give good advice when it is our friend in trouble instead of us. Think about what you would say to your friend who might be in the same difficult situation you face. After clearly picturing your friend in the situation, picture and feel what you would say to him. You'll notice that when you offer advice, you are feeling no stress, just compassion and concern for your friend. It is your personal involvement that creates the stress and the difficult feelings. Offering the advice to "someone else" removes the personal involvement. Now turn and say the same thing to yourself! Become your own friend.

We also make mistakes when we are personally and emotionally involved. If you examine your own life, you'll find that all the choices you made that you came to regret were made when you were heavily personally and emotionally involved. When we're the observer, we see clearly and don't make the kind of mistakes we regret later. It is our wishing things to be different, regretting that they aren't, and acting as if they were, that results in poor choices being made.

Being Passive Is Not the Answer

There is nothing in what has been said so far that is intended to be an exhortation to be passive. Far from it. The firefighters, police forces, U.S. military, hospital emergency room technicians, and other emergency personnel we have trained need to move quickly. How is this possible, given that we have suggested stepping back and watching the "movie?"

Suppose there is a situation where someone is particularly rude to you. You take a step back and look at a movie of the scene. You are now looking at a movie of two people, one of whom is being intimidated and bullied by a rude person. I say to you, "What do you think should happen in that movie? How should the recipient of this bullying behavior respond?" You, as a spectator to this movie, may answer that you think the bully needs to be shouted down. That it's the only thing he'll hear, and that it's the best thing to happen. Well, if that's your decision, go for it! There is no suggestion to be passive here. This book is not named "Doormat 101." All we are saying is that whatever your choice, whether to let it go or stand up and fight, it must come from free will and not be governed by your personal and emotional reaction.

No specific *behavior* is ruled out here, just behavior stemming from an emotional reaction. The question is not what we *do*, but whether we are feeling *free* and making a *choice* when we do it, or reacting out of compulsion because "I can't stand it when . . ." If you can't stand it, the problem of being "unable to stand it" is yours, and the "standing it" part has to do with your abilities, not the situation.

There are two separate and somewhat independent realities going on here. One is what is happening externally, and we can make all sorts of true statements about it: He is a bully. His behavior is inappropriate. He does this all the time. He was brought up poorly. These are true statements and are not "stress."

The second reality is how we respond to that state of affairs: I hate it when he does that. I feel weak and defenseless when he does that. I get angry when he does that. These statements are about what is happening inside us and are only true because of how we feel. Fortunately, these feelings are created by our perceptions, and our perceptions can be changed.

Furthermore, if you step back and look at the movie, you will also know what the best course of action is. After all, what is the chance of your emotional reaction being the very best thing to do in a difficult situation? Virtually zero. But what are the chances you'd make the right choice if you step back and look at the movie? Pretty darn good. You'd give good advice if it were happening to someone else. You'd also know what to do a week later. Well, make the week later now! In fact, the only time we *don't* know what to do is when we're personally and emotionally involved because it's at those times that we do not see straight. Once you have cleared your mind and are free, you can do whatever you think is best with confidence.

A friend and colleague of mine has been working with this idea for many years. She shared a personal experience of hers, and I will share it as it was told to me.

> I was working with a woman who had a tendency to become overbearing when deadlines loomed or other pressures mounted. I dislike conflict and would always just speak more softly hoping to appease her and mute her outbursts. Instead, each concession just encouraged her to push for more from me. This increased pushing would lead to more concessions on my part, and the cycle of pushing and yielding would eventually go way too far.

> One day, at the first sign of the objectionable overbearing behavior, I was finally able to take a mental step back. I viewed the situation in my mind as if it involved two other people and could then see what was needed.

> I immediately said, "No. I'm afraid I'm not able to do what you want." She angrily asked why, and I simply raised my own voice and energy enough to meet the challenge head-on. A heated dialogue ensued, but at least it was a dialogue. After a short time we were able to work out our differences. The problem was much easier for me to handle after that, and even arose less frequently. Apparently, what I finally came to see was true: that standing up to her was what was needed.

The woman's emotional reaction of wanting to "quiet things down" simply resulted in an endless cycle of pushing and yielding. When we do what we do because we just can't stand doing it any other way, we are trapped by our own likes and dislikes. We thus don't see a large number of possibilities, one of which might actually be the best approach to solving the problem. Our emotional involvement prevents us from seeing other alternatives.

Getting the Ball Is Not Stress

This stepping-back process does not leave us being passive, however. Suppose you were playing tennis with a friend, and the tennis ball was hit to the far side of the court. Would you throw your racket down and say, "Why did you hit it over there? When I was standing over there, you hit it over here. So I ran here, and now you hit it back over there. I hate this — it's so unfair!" Instead of complaining, you'd just run to get the ball. You understand that wishing the ball were elsewhere is not helpful. Complaining about the unfairness of its location is also not helpful.

We are not suggesting that you fail to get the ball. This is about not wishing it were elsewhere. Go get the ball! In fact, the energy we put into mentally wishing the ball were elsewhere is exactly how much less energy we have to actually get the ball.

"Getting the ball" is what it's all about. Wishing the ball were elsewhere, complaining about the ball, looking for whose fault it is that the ball is somewhere where you can't hit it, worrying about the ball, and feeling unworthy about your ability to get the ball, are all quite beside the point and will actually interfere with getting the ball. Stepping back mentally in order to quiet the mind, as we are suggesting, will make you much more effective and dynamic rather than passive because your energy is going into what needs to be done rather than into thinking about what you like or don't like, regret or don't regret, or can or can't stand.

Suppose you are skiing and the ski slope goes to the left. Would you say, "I hate turning left. My father was always trying to teach me to turn left when he taught me how to ski because I'm right-handed, and I hated my father. To spite him, I never learned, so now I only turn right when I ski." This approach is not recommended, especially if the slope you're on veers to the left! We yell at the movie when we feel we desperately *need* the world to be different.

Imagine watching a martial artist on stage at a demonstration. He stands there poised and relaxed when suddenly six men with knives rush at him from off stage. In a flash all six men are disarmed and are on the floor. What he doesn't do as they approach is think, "Hey! They told me there would only be five guys in rehearsal. I hate it when this happens! It's so unfair. Who's responsible for this?" There is no time for such nonsense.

I was booked to present our program for the staff of a small company. They had arranged for it to be off-site at a country club and had secured a small building for us to use. I arrived early to set up and discovered that the door of the building was locked. I had been told that it would be open, and that the property's facilities manager would be available by phone should I need him. I called both his number as well as the one for the main reception area, but there was no answer at either as it was quite early in the morning. No one seemed to be around, and the building was quite some distance from any other. Just then a couple of attendees arrived, and I shared what had been going on. They were from the company that had booked us and knew nothing about the locked building. I made another call or two but to no avail. A few more people came, but still no one could help. It started to drizzle lightly.

By now about half the attendees were there, and they had broken into small groups outside the building. As a student of human nature, it was very interesting to watch what was developing. Like-minded people always find each other. One group was complaining about whoever it was that dropped the ball and caused this glitch. Another was talking about how unlucky they were and how these sorts of things always happened to them. A third group was saying that if they had been in charge, this never would have happened. But not one person was "getting the ball!"

At this point it seemed likely that no help was going to come. I walked around the building and, as it was just a one story building, I looked for a window that had not been secured. I assumed that since it was summer, they were opened every day and there'd be a reasonable chance one might be unlocked, and sure enough one was. I climbed in easily and opened the front door. Everyone filed in and most continued their conversations about blame.

IV

PROGRESS IS DIRECTIONAL

I hope you understand that I myself am not perfect at any of the practices I have described (far from it!). But I've devoted my life to getting better at them.

It's important to understand that these changes of attitude and behavior we are discussing are directional. The question is not whether you can do this perfectly and in all circumstances, but whether you are moving in the direction of being able to do this in an ever growing number of situations. That is, will you be better at this next month than this month? And will you be better six months from now than one month from now? If you focus on directional improvement rather than some imagined state of perfection, you will see tangible benefits and be able to take satisfaction in your progress immediately.

The fortunate thing about practicing these ideas and unlike so many other things we undertake is that the benefit is immediate. Suppose someone decides to go on a diet and eats carefully for a whole day. At the end of the day he runs to the scale to weigh himself. You can be sure that there won't be much to rejoice about. Weighing yourself after a little practice of your new eating regimen will not show much improvement, so continuing on is more of an act of faith and willpower. With the changes and techniques we are discussing, however, there is immediate and instant improvement. The quick positive results often help us see the value of what we are doing and encourage us to continue to make progress. I mentioned one attendee who was able to get rid of her migraines in short order by practicing what she had learned. You can be sure that she kept up her practice! Anything is better than the tremendous pain associated with migraines.

Start With a Two-pound Weight

Nothing that has been said so far is intended to imply that stepping back is easy to do in every circumstance. It isn't and I'm quite familiar with what it feels like to have my mind and feelings out of control. If I were walking somewhere with my wife, Karen, and saw her get hit by a car, my response would most definitely not be, "Oh, what an interesting movie!" It would be enormously difficult to avoid being personally and emotionally involved with that circumstance.

Let's look at the things we face in terms of weights. Something awful like that might be the equivalent of a 300-pound weight for me. How do we learn to lift a 300-pound weight? We start by practicing with a two-pound weight, then after a while we go up to a five-pound weight, then later a ten-pound weight and so on.

So too with this process. We start by controlling our responses in little situations – our two-pound weights. A two-pound weight is defined as something that bothers you just a little bit. A two-pound weight is not something you think *ought* to bother you just a little bit. Nor is it something that bothers *most* people just a little bit. It is something that actually bothers *you* just a little bit.

I'd like to give you a homework assignment: The next time a little thing comes up (a two-pound weight), don't react to it. You will have hundreds of opportunities to practice this every day. But what might a two-pound weight look like?

We were presenting a program, and I had just given this assignment when we took a short break. One of the people in the class shared this story with me as soon as she returned from the break:

> You had just said we should start practicing by not reacting to two-pound weights, and I didn't quite see what you meant. As I was mulling it over, I walked toward the table with the small bottles of water on it. I reached for one, still puzzling about what a two-pound weight might look like, and as I grabbed a water, I realized it was warm. Reaching for another I realized that they were all warm! My first thought was, "Who the heck was dumb enough to put out warm water?" I immediately smiled and thought, "Oh, there's a two-pound weight!" I never would have noticed what I had done had you not just spoken about how we complain at the movie in little ways hundreds of times a day.

It is almost impossible to resist focusing on our 200-pound weights. After all, that's why you are reading this book: to deal with your most difficult situations, not your easiest-to-handle problems. You probably didn't buy this book to figure out how to cope with the stress created when you break your shoelace! But we need to retrain ourselves, break our habits, and build some new mental muscles. No one goes to a gym and says to the trainer: "This is my first day here, and I've come to develop some upper body strength. Let's get started. Where's your heaviest barbell?" We know progress is made in small increments starting with lighter weights, so we can build up our strength. The difficulty is that we really want to start with our biggest challenges. Nevertheless, you are most likely to be successful with this process if you make progress over time by starting with something you can actually handle.

But the mind is stubborn and you're probably still thinking about your own 200-pound weights. It can be all right to start there, so long as you understand that it's extracurricular. It won't hurt you to try what we have described on your 200-pound weight. It's just not a good idea to start with a too-heavy weight, to be unable to step back and choose your response, and to conclude that this approach isn't realistic because you couldn't do it where and when you wanted to.

If you walked into a room and someone asked you to lift a piano, you might even give it a try, but you would undoubtedly be unable to lift it. Yet you wouldn't conclude that your muscles had failed. You would just figure, "Well, I may not be able lift the piano, but I can certainly lift the bench next to it." The same is true here. Start with what you *can* lift and thereby build up your strength and confidence. This will ensure that over time you will be able to lift larger and larger weights. That is, be inwardly free from emotional and personal attachments in increasingly difficult situations. Starting with smaller challenges will also give you a feel for what successful application looks like.

If you are unable to step back and watch the movie in a given situation, it simply means that you are starting with something that is over your head. Find a situation that is more suitable until you get the hang of how to step back properly.

We Each React Differently to the Same Situation

When starting with a two-pound weight, understand that there is no external, objective list of weights. Different people evaluate identical situations differently. Just because a situation is a two-pound weight for *you* doesn't mean it would be the same for everyone, or even anyone. Conversely, what seems like a fifty-pound weight for you might be almost nothing to someone else. Remember, the level of the weight (whether it is two or two hundred pounds) is solely a question of how much it bothers you.

I remember one time during a program I was asking people to name situations that they were facing that they felt stressed about. People were volunteering an unfortunately common list of serious difficulties: divorce, money problems, health challenges, etc. One woman sitting in the front suddenly raised her hand with real determination. It seemed as if she were ready to share her personal 200-pound weight. I called on her and she virtually exploded with, "Bank fees!" There were a number of titters in the room. I asked her to explain. She said, "I have a young niece, and I like to give her a small gift every few months or so. I don't have much money myself, but I want to teach her the value of saving, so I opened up a savings account for her. Because it's a small account and I only put in $10 at a time, the bank debits $3 a month as a maintenance fee, and it drives me crazy!"

Everyone had stopped giggling, but I could tell there still wasn't much sympathy in the room. I said, "Don't laugh. We all have things that drive us crazy. Is it really much more sensible to be infuriated with the fellow who pulls in front of us on the highway? What does it actually cost us? Two seconds because we have to slow down?"

Sometimes people say, "There's this little thing that drives me crazy." This is an inappropriate phrase. If it's driving you crazy, for you it's not a little thing. Just because it's little to most people doesn't mean a thing as far as you're concerned. When we say to start with a two-pound weight we mean something that feels like two pounds to *you.*

Let's face it: we're all a bit odd. We just hang around with other people who are odd like us, and then we think we're normal. There are people who are free spirits and artists. They hang around with each other and look at the people who are very organized and think, "Boy, are they uptight. What a bunch of Type 'A's.' They'll probably all have heart attacks before they're fifty."

The organized people are probably looking at the artists thinking, "Boy, are they dreamers. They're so disorganized and carefree, they'll probably never amount to anything." We spend time with people like ourselves because that makes us more comfortable. Our group then assumes that everyone else is missing the point somehow.

We're all a bit odd because our behavior is primarily driven by our hopes and fears. Only when we are free to choose, will we have gained the ability to see someone else clearly. They may be missing *our* point, but our point is simply based on our oddities instead of theirs! Emotional freedom gives us the ability to see what is true as opposed to what we conclude after it goes through our own prejudicial filters.

Once free, we tend to be much less judgmental because we see people for who and what they are. We don't judge them based on the filter of what *we* like and need. Remember how we had compassion for the blind person who bumped us on the bus rather than finding fault? Seeing his blindness helped us change perspective from ourselves to him. Just changing our focus from how we disliked what he did to us to his reality immediately resulted in our stepping back.

But How do You Deal With a 200-pound Weight?

What should you do when a 200-pound weight shows up and you have to deal with it? If you've practiced these techniques and attitudes in the many two, five, and ten-pound weights you face every day, you'll be starting from a position of strength. You will have had a good day and be feeling great when the heavy weight shows up. Taking an obvious physical example, if you knew you were going to have a very long day coming up, you might want to rest the day before to ensure you'd be strong enough for the hectic pace to come. In the same way, if you knew that you were going to have a stressful event come up soon, you might want to make sure that your stress resistance level was in top shape before the big event came. The best way to do this is to practice those techniques discussed in earlier chapters in all the lesser situations (the two- and ten-pound weights) so that when the big one arrives, you're strong and smiling at the start.

When a big one is upon you, just try stepping back and watching the movie anyway. Unlike lifting physical weights, trying something that seems too big for you will not cause you harm if you're unable to lift it. And sometimes we can get a little lucky and hoist a large one. It's similar to the stories we have all heard about a small mother who sees a heavy object fall over onto her infant. Suddenly, with an unknown burst of strength, she lifts the weight to free the child. Afterwards even she doesn't know where the strength came from. We sometimes find ourselves in a situation that might be expected to be way over our heads, yet we react with calm and grace. Practicing ahead of time and becoming completely comfortable with these ideas significantly increases the chances that we will surprisingly lift that large-sized stressor that has just entered our lives. There is no harm in trying, so long as you remember not to get discouraged if the 200-pound weight is more than you can handle.

V

CHANGE AND STRESS

W e tend to fear change out of concern that a coming change may somehow threaten us. Yet many times, change is not only welcomed but sought after. If we were to ski the same downhill run every day of a long ski trip, we'd become bored. If the tennis ball were hit to the same spot each time, we would find the game much less interesting after a short while and would probably just quit playing. It is not knowing what's coming next that makes the game interesting. We enjoy putting ourselves into sporting situations where the whole point is to adapt quickly. We even pay money to be able to have these experiences.

Why not take the same approach to life? When you wake up in the morning, determine to ski through your day. If your day goes to the left, lean and turn left. If your day goes to the right, lean and turn right. If the tennis ball is hit perfectly into the far corner and beyond your reach, just smile and say inwardly, "Nice shot, Day. But I'll get the next one. You can't beat me. Bring it on!"

You can't be beaten unless you agree to be beaten. The real game – the important game – is not about the points on the court but is entirely about our inner response to the shots that we cannot return. We lose when we blame the shot. We lose when we feel defeated. We lose when we complain the shot wasn't fair. We lose when we say, "Why me?" (which of course begs the question, "Why *not* you?") We lose when we get angry at the ball, the size of the court, or the other player. In short, we lose whenever we forget that the entire game is about our response to the situation. We must step back, decide whether the ball is returnable, and run like lightning if it is, or just let it pass and move on to the next point if it is not.

In time we come to see that gaining control over our responses is the best game there is, with the most challenge and by far the greatest level of reward for victory or, alternately, the greatest cost for defeat. And fortunately, mastering this inner game will make it infinitely more likely that you will be able to score outer points as well. Remember, the energy you put into wishing the ball were elsewhere is energy you don't have to get the ball.

We all face serious difficulties from time to time, and we don't mean to minimize them. And those minor difficulties certainly seem to have the power to upset us. But to the extent that we determine to face our circumstances appropriately, they cease to have the power over us that stems entirely from the power we ourselves give them. Their existence in our lives may be something we cannot alter, but the effect they have on us can be changed by the mental attitudes we adopt.

As when we put a hand on a hot stove and suffer the consequences, the choice of our attitudes can lead to pain.

The choice of attitude is up to us, and the instant we decide that we've had enough of getting burned, the cycle can begin to end. Unfortunately, the consequences of the attitude choices we make are not as obvious as they are when we touch the stove. It is this disconnect and delay that allows us to continue to keep our damaging attitudes without feeling the immediate pain that touching a hot stove brings us. This is why it is necessary to see the connection between "attitude" and "pain" through discrimination, understanding, and self-examination. We need to develop the same reaction to "yelling at the movie" that a child has when it hears the words, "No! Hot!" from his mother. We have been "burned" but simply do not identify being personally and emotionally involved as the cause of our pain.

A friend of mine is quite adept at practicing these principles. The attitudes and perspectives we have been sharing have simply become a natural part of him over the years. His ability in this area was made clear by a series of circumstances with which he was involved some years ago.

My friend was traveling to vacation on Lake Tahoe with some of his friends when his car got into an accident with a bus. No one was injured, but the car was disabled and could not be driven. After making the proper arrangements for it to be towed, it turned out that the bus itself was heading to Tahoe as well. The small group simply took their luggage and continued on for their vacation.

One of the passengers on the bus, who of course had witnessed the events, said to my friend, "Your car just got wrecked, yet you look as if nothing had happened. Don't you care?" His response was both remarkable and interesting:

"Of course I care, but I figure that a year from now what just happened won't bother me. If that is so, then why should I waste a year being upset about it? I choose not to be upset right now."

So many difficult experiences that happen to us make great stories later, and we often relish talking and even laughing about them. Well, why not laugh now? The events that transpired do not change simply because it's a year later. The only thing that has changed in the intervening year is our attitude about them, and our attitude can be influenced by our own perceptions, will, and effort. Why allow them to hurt us until the pain simply wears off a year later?

We Are Free to Choose and Act

If we are acting out of compulsion and an "I-hate-it-when-that-happens" attitude, we are basically in a position of slavery. Our mood and consciousness are completely under the control of other people or external circumstances. If people are nice to me, I have a good day. If not, I have a bad one. If my car is working, I'm happy. If not, I'm sad. If I have enough money, I'm happy. If not, I'm sad. If I'm too fat, or too thin, or balding, or in a bad relationship, or have to travel, or can never travel. . . . The list goes on and on. Needing our circumstances to be just right for us to feel happy and content means that we are always slaves to those circumstances. And even when things are going well, we're afraid the situation is "too good to last."

Sometimes when I present this program, I stop and, sweeping the audience with my eyes, say:

Right now everyone in this room is my slave. I can change the mood of anyone I choose. If I walked right up to you and said, "Your presence is ruining the whole program. Get out!" I bet your mood would change! You'd either become angry or embarrassed, depending on your personality, but your mood would certainly change as a result of my comment. Why be a slave to my behavior? You don't even know me. I'm not even the real instructor. The instructor is tied up in the trunk of my car. I'm just some nut who wanders into classes and abuses people! You're a free person. There is nothing forcing you to react to any of my words or actions. Just watch a "movie" of a man behaving inappropriately.

I'm not perfect at any of this, but since the real goal is directional improvement, I can say I am much better at it than I used to be. Let's experiment. Right now, anyone in this room, go for it – insult me! I'll just look at you like you're a movie. Why should I allow your comments to affect me? To be honest, if you are really good at insults, I may have to look at you as if you were in a horror movie! But more likely I'll just look at it as if it were a comedy. Why must I be affected by your strange behavior? I challenge anyone in here to show me the causality – the physics level of causality – between how you behave and how I have to feel.

But Don't Situations Cause Stress?

Suppose you watch a boat sail on a river towards a drawbridge. Every day you sit on the bank, watch the boat approach the drawbridge, and see the bridge go up. The boat passes underneath and, after clearing the bridge, the bridge lowers again.

If you had just dropped in from another planet and didn't know how these things worked, it would be very likely that you would believe that the boat somehow caused the bridge to move. In fact, however, there is a man in a control booth at the base of the bridge who, upon seeing the approaching boat, pushes the right buttons and pulls the right levers to get the bridge to rise.

Our reaction to difficult situations is very much the same. We believe that situations somehow "cause" stress, when in fact the circumstances are just a trigger. Something happens and we feel stress (the bridge goes up). The man in the booth working the bridge controls is our mind. If we can get the man in the booth to behave differently, the bridge does not *have* to go up. It is a choice he is making – in the case of the coming boat, a good one! – but a choice nonetheless.

The man at the controls is not totally beyond our will and influence. As we practice, we find that the link of causality – that situations "create" and "cause" our stress – begins to melt away. The situation is just a trigger that results in the man at the controls responding in a certain way. Through practice we can get him (our minds) to respond in a different way. Rather than thinking that we need the situation to be different, we can act on the mind directly. The situation can remain exactly the same, but if we can change our perceptions, we can avoid the suffering. (Are you thinking, "How can I ever do this with my situation?" If so, you are probably thinking about your 200-pound weight. If this is happening to you, start smaller!)

This is good news because we may not be able to influence the approach of the boat, but we can ultimately have tremendous influence over the behavior of the man in the booth. Our behavior depends on our perception of the things around us and their level of threat to us, our beliefs about the level of danger they represent, our thoughts about the harm they may cause, and much more. In other words, our perceptions determine our degree of stress, but we can influence our perceptions in a positive way through practice. This introduces a powerful weapon against stress: control. Feeling out of control induces stress, while feeling in control is a tremendous weapon in defeating stress.

Stress and Control

An experiment was done in which two mice were placed in a cage. The floor was very mildly electrified, just enough to be a small irritation. The cage was divided in half by a wall. The mice were as genetically identical as possible as were their conditions. The only difference was that one mouse had a lever in his half that would turn off the mild shock when pressed. When that mouse felt the shock, it learned to hit the lever in order to turn it off. Since the electricity would go off for both halves, the mice had identical physical experiences.

The results of this setup were both revealing and important. The mouse with the lever in his half of the cage showed an increase of stress. He was obviously not a happy mouse. But the other mouse showed a much greater level of stress. Why? They were experiencing the exact same physical sensations. But the mouse with the lever had some control and exercised it. The stress on the second mouse was caused by his feeling out of control.

Our mistake as humans, though, is seeking to control the wrong thing. We think we should be able to control our circumstances when in fact it is often our own attitudes and perceptions that we can ultimately influence and control. Once those are under our command, we can turn our clear and effective mind towards the circumstances we seek to alter.

Being unable to control something – even something we'd like to be different – does not in itself create stress. It is our thwarted *desire* to control something that creates stress. Let's see how this is true.

Yelling at the Movie Prevents Us From Solving Problems

A woman shared the following story when approaching me after attending our program:

> My husband and I just moved to this area. We bought a big house. There's no furniture in it. He knows, as I do, that we need furniture. For the last two weeks we've practically been eating on the floor. He simply doesn't want to go with me to shop for furniture. He keeps saying, "Just get whatever you want." This would be fine except he is also incredibly picky, so I know what's going to happen. I'm going to come home with a whole truck full of furniture, and I'm going to have to listen to him endlessly tell me how much he doesn't like any of it. The last time something like this happened he complained about it for years. This whole situation is driving me crazy.

I decided the best approach for her was for us to practice the "stepping back and watching the movie" exercise.

I said to her, "Come over here," and standing side by side I pointed to the wall and said, "Let's say we're looking at a movie. The heroine of the movie is not you, it's some other woman. She's with her husband in a new house with no furniture and they need to get furniture." I then proceeded to describe the situation in which she found herself, including the personality of her husband that I gave to the husband in the "movie." I emphasized to her that it was not she in the movie, but some other woman.

I asked her what the woman in the movie should do about the situation, and she immediately said, "Well, I think I should . . ." I interrupted and said, "It's not you in the movie. It's someone else. Why did you say "I?" When we are dealing with a 100-pound weight it's harder to take that step back and become the observer, and this situation was quite hard for her. After I worked with her for a while, she was able to get enough distance from her own situation to feel as though she were watching a movie of someone else. Once I was sure she had attained the necessary degree of separation, I pointed at the blank wall where the movie was being "shown" and said, "Now I have a question for you. Given the character of the man in that movie, do you think that the guy in the movie is ever going to go shopping with that woman?" Right away she said, "No way!"

I continued, "I have another question for you. How do you feel about what you just discovered – that he's never going to go?" She replied, with a slight sense of surprise in her voice, "It doesn't bother me quite as much."

After going through this exercise with the woman, several very interesting things happened. The first was that with considerable surprise she said to me, "You know,

I feel like I'm seeing my husband for who he really is for the first time. He's not going to go! He's simply not wired that way!" I then said, "Yes, and I bet you'd really like it if he were six-foot-four. Then he could change all the light bulbs in the house without getting a ladder. And I'll bet his height doesn't bother you either. Or he could be rich. That would be great, but his not being rich doesn't bother you either. In fact there are lots of ways he could be different, each of which you would prefer, and none of which bother you. Why not just add 'doesn't do furniture shopping' to the pile?"

The next thing that happened surprised me and was even more interesting. She suddenly said, "Hey! I know how I can get him to go! There's a hardware store where he always wants me to go. It's got a lot of high-tech gadgets that he thinks are great that I couldn't be less interested in. He's always wanting me to go check it out with him, and I always refuse the invitation. But it's just a block from a furniture store. I'll bet anything that if I go with him to his store, he'd come with me to the furniture store down the street when we're done."

I asked her why a solution suddenly occurred to her and hadn't before. She confessed that for the previous two weeks, all she had been doing was yelling at the movie. Her entire focus was on how *he* should be different. No thought at all was given to actually solving the problem. With the mindset she had, the only problem she could see was that he was a cad, and that if only he were different, the problem would be solved and she could be happy again. Once we learn to step back and look at the movie, we see solutions where we previously saw only problems. We can then focus on what to do to make things better rather than how everyone else, or everything else, should be different.

Once you've stepped back, if you really feel that things should be different, do something about it! It's the mind that causes our stress. Remember the experiment with the mice? Feeling out of control is a key component of stress.

No One Can Fly

Wouldn't it be great if we could fly by just flapping our arms? It sure would! Fresh air, no traffic, no need for gasoline, good exercise, and no more car insurance. But who wakes up in the morning, jumps out of bed, flaps his arms, and with real disappointment thinks, "Darn! I still can't fly!" It would be great if you could fly, and you'll just never be able to. Why doesn't this bother you? Because you simply accept the fact that you can't fly. If all your friends could fly, you'd be irritated. Frustration is never a question of not having something that would be great. It's a question of whether we *expect* to be able to have it.

A woman told me a marvelous story some years ago.

> My husband and I had a big three-story house. We lived there with our four-year-old son who was quite an energetic and strong-willed little boy. One night at 2 a.m. we awoke to a noise. He had gotten out of his bed and walked to the top of the stairs. His shout could be heard throughout the house. Shaking his little fist at the sky he cried, "I want it to be day!"

It's funny and endearing when a child shouts at reality informing it that it had better shape up. It's less endearing as adults, so we do it mentally instead, but with the same effectiveness as the child.

We Can Choose Our Response

You can choose your response in any circumstance. You may not be in a position to exercise control over the circumstances in which you find yourself, but you can always influence what is happening inside you. Focusing on choosing your response will result in seeing solutions, while at the same time allowing you to feel in control, which is in itself an antidote for stress. We are simply too often seeking to control the wrong things. Just turn the mirror around. You are probably pointing it in the wrong direction!

I'm not letting the other person off the hook. It's not as if I'm saying that someone's poor behavior is fine if it isn't. It's just that to focus on his behavior before getting your own house in order maximizes the chance for our own inappropriate response. We feel stress because we continue to think or say that "If only *he* were different, then I could be happy" (and if only that were different, and that, and that, and so on . . .). We thus become slaves to our circumstances, a surefire recipe for stress.

Here again we see why this is not an exhortation to be passive. Focusing on our inner response does not prohibit any needed action on our part. There is nothing "meek" about the acceptance of reality. This kind of dynamic acceptance is not to be confused with giving up or some kind of self-denying compromising.

Compromising and Giving Up

If we see reality for what it actually is, which can only happen when we are free and no longer personally and emotionally involved, we feel no sense of "giving up." We are not giving up on our desire to fly. We simply see that it is not in the cards and accept reality. Are there other people in your life you wish were different? Will they really change, or are you just wishing they would? If we see the other person for whom he really is, and can see what we hope for is in fact unlikely or impossible, we're not compromising. If, on the other hand, they really can do what we want them to, then let's get them to do it.

If you are working with a small child, you know what to expect. If you want the child to help you balance your checkbook, you'll be disappointed. Accepting that the child cannot help, even though you just made his lunch, is neither giving up nor compromising. Giving up has a sense of unfairness to it – that you have somehow been defeated. Dynamic acceptance has a sense of victory, for you've been able to see reality for what it is and have mastered your own reactive process.

Why Lose Twice?

A woman who attended one of our programs had a realization during the class and said:

> Just as you were speaking I realized how annoyed I was when getting on the highway. Every time I drove someplace there would be one or two instances of someone doing something that would make me mad.

The incident would last for just a second, but it would stick in my mind the whole time I was out. Suddenly I could see how this meant I was losing twice every time something happened. The first "loss" was unavoidable and occurred when someone cut me off or prevented me from turning where I needed to go. This loss normally cost me about two seconds! But the second loss lasted far longer and was much worse. It was all the time I spent holding onto what had happened. I can see now how ridiculous that is and how I simply don't need to do that anymore. I don't think I'll ever be completely o.k. with what other people do on the road, but I also don't think it will ever again torment me like it used to.

VI

REACTING VS. RESPONDING

When one takes a drug and the medication causes a problem, the phrase often used is the patient had a "negative reaction." If the drug does its job without incident, one might hear that the patient is "responding" to treatment. The negative and positive aspects of these two words can be used in a similar way for our purposes. When we "react" to a situation, we are out of control and will likely face unfortunate consequences. Instead, when we "respond," we are thoughtful, centered, and clear-minded while still doing what needs to be done. Emergency personnel are sometimes called an "emergency response team." No one in danger wants an "emergency react team!" Action is present in both cases, showing that neither route suggests passivity, but the action taken by someone who is choosing his response is far superior to action taken by one who is reacting based on their fears, needs, or strong desires.

Get Off Drugs Before You Act

When we are feeling stress, it's as if we are on drugs. Our entire body chemistry is out of whack, with different chemicals racing through our blood stream and affecting how we think and behave. We must get off the drugs before we do anything. It's as if we were about to perform delicate brain surgery and decided to take a mind-altering drug before starting the surgery! First, get off the drugs (reduce the stress level), and *then* decide how to proceed. Quieting the stress first does not rule out any behavior nor, as we shall see a little later, slow us down or cause us to miss opportunities.

We think we have many roles and jobs: father, mother, friend, citizen, parent, spouse, teacher, lawyer, salesperson, etc. But in fact we have one most important job and it may not be the one we think we have. Our one job – our top priority – is to regain control of our own reactive process. Once this is accomplished, every other task we undertake and every personal relationship of any kind will be significantly improved. Having conquered the part of us that is currently out of control, we can apply our minds and intentions to whatever we want and will have notably greater success. It all starts with what is happening within our own minds and not with external circumstances. Dealing with the circumstances will come, but not until *after* we ourselves are under control.

If, in a difficult situation, your first thought is, "Well, he shouldn't have . . ." or "That shouldn't be that way . . ." you've already lost. Our first thought needs to be what is happening between our own ears. Once we get that right we have earned the right to look outside ourselves. Until then, we are simply slaves to our circumstances and other people's behavior.

Why Is This So Hard To Do?

It is interesting that the practices and attitudes encouraged here seem to run completely counter to what our society tells us. Every day we are bombarded by advertisements that say, "If only you'd use this toothpaste, you'd find the life partner you want and be really happy," or, "If only you'd use this type of laundry detergent, your family would love you so much more, and *then* real happiness could finally be yours." I have always marveled at the typical scene in a household product commercial. A woman is cleaning her floor with the latest product, and she seems so happy, as if the cleanser were somehow a life-fulfillment. And if using the right household cleanser won't bring us the joy we seek in life, surely the new car featured in the next ad will.

Years ago, when Karen and I decided to move to Silicon Valley and start Clarity Seminars, we realized that we would need an upgraded computer setup to launch our new enterprise. We were understandably excited as we are both facile with computers and getting the newest whiz-bangs was sure to be fun.

We spent many hours researching to figure out exactly what our needs would be and what system would meet them for the best price. Finally, we made the decision and placed the order. A few days later, the shipment arrived. Karen, being more of a computer enthusiast than I, tore open the box first and felt a great upsurge of happiness just seeing our new toy. She had what we had been re-searching and wanting for so long. Now we could start our new enterprise on the right foot. Now nothing could hold us back! But this great sense of excitement lasted about thirty seconds. She very soon realized that it was just an-other thing. She smiled to herself thinking, "Caught again."

The joy that came to her after that recognition was much stronger and deeper than the feeling that accompa-nied opening the box. The feeling of freedom always is, knowing deeply that one's happiness is not dependent on a box or a material good that will grow old and eventually gather dust and break. Lasting joy is dependent on the deep sense of freedom that comes from a life of centered de-tachment. This is not about feeling less or being unable to enjoy the good things that come to us as we will soon see.

This drive to alter our circumstances is not only per-fectly natural but is also the basis for capitalism. The images that western culture now presents were not "in-vented" to spur purchasing. They developed because they resonate with something deep in human nature. It takes very little to convince us that if we just had "more" we'd be happier. The more we get, the happier we are supposed to be. This is generally believed on some deep level in spite of the many people who "have it all" but are clearly unhappy. "Having it all" is not enough if the "all" does not include our own minds.

We Can Improve On Nature

Sometimes people say, "Well, if looking to change our circumstances before we change ourselves is natural, what's the big deal?" Our bodies are created in a certain state, but through exercise and working out, we can improve what nature has given us. Working with our attitudes is no different. We are often brought up with attitudes and beliefs that are not helpful in getting us where we want to go. Through practice, however, we can correct these mistaken notions just as we can improve our bodies through exercise. Just because we were born with certain mental tendencies does not mean that we cannot work to change these natural beliefs.

Feelings vs. Emotions

We've spent much time explaining how stress is a function of being personally and emotionally involved with what is happening around us. We have shown how taking a step back gives us clarity but does not result in our becoming passive. The gifted martial artist, for example, is clear and centered, but when the time is right, he is anything but passive and moves like lightning. Yet you may still be wondering whether the world we have thus far described might be dull or uninteresting in which you might feel calmer but are not attracted to because so many of life's enjoyments have been drained from it.

Actually, just the opposite is true. By practicing the attitudes we have been encouraging, we wind up feeling *more* of the feelings we value most, not less. Joy, compassion, love, and enthusiasm are a few of the feelings that are enhanced through the process of stepping back. This is because there is an important difference between "feelings" and "emotions." Feelings, such as the positive ones we have just mentioned, are pure and undistorted, and life would not be life without them. Emotions stem from feelings, but are quite different. This is best illustrated by example.

Suppose you're at a party and dishes of ice cream are set out on a counter for everyone. You approach the counter and see a nice dish of chocolate, your favorite flavor. A little thought of "Oh, goodie!" flits through your mind. The enjoyment of chocolate is just a feeling, and as such creates no problem (it's a good thing as it'd be hard to imagine giving up chocolate!). Take a dish. Enjoy it fully. No problem.

But suppose that just as you start to approach it, some-one else takes the dish you had targeted. Even worse, scanning the rest of the counter you realize it was the last chocolate ice cream, and the empty container is sitting right there as proof.

If you become disappointed, at that moment your feeling has become an emotion. An emotion is a feeling coupled with a need for the world to be a certain way. "Liking" something is fine. Feeling that you *need* that item or situation to be your way creates a bondage to circum-stances. The stronger the feeling of need, the stronger the bondage, the greater the pain or frustration at its lack, and the greater the stress level. We used the trivial example of ice cream to make the point, but the identical mechanism is in play regardless of the depth of the perceived "need." "I can't be happy unless I get the chocolate, or the new car, or that vacation, or the new job, or more money, or better health, or. . . ." The list goes on infinitely and leads us absolutely nowhere. There is nothing wrong with liking those things. There is not even anything wrong with wanting them. It is our *need* for them that creates the problem. It is our deep but subtle belief that they will somehow make us happier, even though in reality it is our own minds that have that power, not external objects or conditions. In part because even when we finally get them, we are satisfied for a brief time, but then the next thing we "need" enters our mind and the cycle starts over.

Just picture how spoiled children might whine for a new toy. They simply cannot stop crying until it is theirs. You get it for them and they are so happy! But how long does that happiness last? If they are truly spoiled, soon they are crying for the next toy. We can never fill the hole created by these wants. Unfulfilled wants always create pain. We can use the techniques we've been discussing, however, to change our wants. Having our desires and sense of need fall under our control and influence is the key.

Junk Food of Emotion

A further example may give us more insight into the difference between emotions and feeling, and how to enhance the positive feelings we prefer while diminishing the power of the negative emotions. Suppose you had been living on strong-tasting junk food and spicy snacks your whole life. If someone were to offer you a delicately flavored meal made by a fine chef, you'd think it had no taste and was bland. The meal was, in fact, not bland but we had become insensitive to the delicate flavors because we'd have become acclimated to the spicy junk food.

The "junk food" in our consciousness is our emotional reactions to things. The delicately flavored meal is our finer feelings. We can scarcely feel the finer feelings having abused our "taste buds" for so long by overstimulation. True feelings, like compassion, selfless love, the desire to serve, peace, and feeling at home wherever you go, have been blocked by the stronger tasting junk food of anger, desire, fear, worry, and self-doubt.

Once we strip away our emotionally reactive selves we are free to allow the finer feelings to blossom fully since they are no longer overshadowed and shouted down by their baser, ruder cousins.

Most of us are inspired by people like the Dali Lama. Wouldn't it be depressing if he said to a reporter one day, "I'd really be much happier if I just had a new car. I've always wanted a nice convertible." What if Mother Teresa had said that?

They are inspiring precisely because they live for others and do not dwell on their own emotional needs. Yet they do not suffer for this supposed "sacrifice," since all they have really sacrificed is slavery to their own urges and desires. We are unlikely to become as great as these people, but we can certainly move in that direction. To the degree we move in that direction we remove another link in our chain of bondage to circumstances.

Willpower vs. Perception

It has correctly been said that environment is stronger than willpower. What this means is that no matter how much we resolve to do something, if we do not create a supportive environment for the change, we place ourselves at a significant disadvantage. Our willpower takes

constant energy to keep strong. A challenging environment, on the other hand, constantly chips away at our
resolve as water dripping on the ground eventually wears
through even solid rock. If one wants to quit drinking, it is
best not to go into bars. Constant exposure to an environment that encourages behavior contrary to what we want
eventually wears us down.

This raises the question of what kind of environment
we create for ourselves. Are our friends reactive? Do they
exude the kind of peace we want for ourselves? Do we
create space in our day, or have we packed our schedule
so tightly that we are always rushing from one thing to
another? If we really want more peace, are we willing to
give up something we think we "need" to create it? Do we
try to "have it all" and lose too much? Isn't peace a part of
that "all" that we want to have? What kind of music do
we listen to? Is it soothing or agitating? Do we drink a lot
of coffee with its agitating caffeine? Do we watch too
much television with its frantic scenes changing every few
seconds? All of these things may disquiet the mind and
may create an environment that is not supportive of the
kind of life we would like. Many of these distractions may
seem necessary, but we must understand and accept that,
like the laws of physics, every choice we make has a consequence. In an important sense you *can* have it all, but
only if you start by owning your own mind first.

Without internal self-control we are constructing a
building with a poorly designed foundation. If the foundation is slanted a touch to the left, the first floor has to be
off a bit to the right to compensate, and then the second
floor is off in the other direction to compensate for the
first floor. Soon our whole misshapen structure collapses

in a nervous breakdown or stress-related problem. Creating the proper environment for ourselves and paying attention to our surroundings will help set that foundation in concrete rather than sand.

We can create a supportive environment, but even that is often not enough unless our perceptions change. Perception is more powerful than willpower.

Suppose you have a weakness for chocolate cake, for example. There is some in your kitchen, but you know you've already had two pieces today and certainly don't need a third. You're sitting in your living room but you can hear it calling to you from the kitchen. You use your willpower to resist eating that third piece, but over time your will may flag, and eventually you approach the cake, bent on its demise. Suppose, however, filled with anticipation, you open the lid and are aghast to see that it's covered with ants. How much willpower does it take to pass up that third piece of cake? None! Once you see those ants it's the easiest thing in the world not to eat it. The changed perception completely removes the need for willpower.

Our attitudes and other habits are like the ants on that cake. If you can come to see how the attitudes we carry cause our stress whenever the world does not do what we want, you'd lose all desire to have those attitudes. In fact, they would disgust you as that ant-covered cake does. If we could come to see the pain inherent in our attitude of needing things our way as clearly as we saw the ants on that cake, we wouldn't have to rely solely on willpower to change. Clarity of perception trumps willpower every time. We would still have habits to break, but the clear perception would make those habits completely unattractive and unmagnetic.

One might liken the situation to how a fan works. When the fan is switched on, the blade is turning with some force. If the plug is pulled, the blade continues to turn, but has no active power behind it and will eventually slow to a complete stop. The blade is our unattractive habit or personal quirk. Once we have seen an undesirable quality of ours for what it is and without denial or defensiveness, we have pulled the plug on it. Habit may keep it turning for a while, but it is receiving no more energy. Eventually it will stop so long as we continue to see it as unwanted and repudiate it.

As we come to see things for what they are, we realize we don't *want* to rush from one thing to another, we don't *want* to spend time with negative or agitating people, and we don't *want* to listen to music that disturbs our peace. Even though these things may seem enjoyable at first, the more clearly we can see the "physics" of the situation – the subtle but direct effect they have on us – the less desirable they will seem to us.

The same is true with our personal flaws. We see the world the way we *want* it to be rather than the way it actually *is*. If we could actually see our flaws as clearly as others see them, we simply would not have them! No one does things that appear unattractive to themselves. It is our lack of clarity of perception that allows the flaws to prosper undisturbed. Once we see them they are eighty percent of the way toward being overcome. This sensitivity to one's personal flaws requires a level of detachment that can be gained by using the techniques we have described.

Change of perception always trumps willpower. This is why some clinics that help people quit smoking often give tours of cancer wards showing people with their larynxes missing, or teenagers are shown movies of maimed car accident victims. The tours and movies are of reality, but the audiences do not want to see the truth in them because it conflicts with the behavior they "enjoy." The more clearly they can see the consequences of their attitudes (the "joys" of driving dangerously or of inhaling poison) the less attractive the actions based on those attitudes become. Once the consequences are clearly seen for what they are, the plug on the fan has been pulled from the socket.

We can become more aware of the damaging influences in our own lives in just the same way: by stepping back and watching the movie. Do we like what we see? Are there changes and suggestions that you, the director, can make in the thoughts and attitudes of the main character that can give us the peace and fulfillment for which we are all searching and so rarely achieve.

The goal of seeing our self-destructive behavior is not to leave us feeling bad, but to have us see this behavior as so unattractive that we simply do not desire it anymore. Denial is not helpful – clear sight is. If from day one a smoker could see his lungs being blackened with every puff, it would be much easier to stop. We need to step back and see what our thoughts and attitudes are doing to us every moment of every day. At first the sight is unpleasant, but the freedom that eventually comes is of far more importance and far more joyful than our desire to blame everything around us instead of our attitudes that are the primary culprit.

VII

SPEED AND STRESS

S peed is becoming a larger and larger factor in modern life. The speed of today's world has many wonderful benefits, but also creates an environment that encourages pressure and stress. If you sent a letter to Europe when America was founded, you wondered what season of the year it would be received. Nowadays, people feel snubbed if they don't receive a response to an email within a few hours. Going to Europe used to take six weeks by boat. Now an eight-hour flight seems like a long time.

It is appropriate and desirable to be able to move fast when it is called for, but it is a sign of poor mental health to be *unable* to slow down. In our speed, we create a sense of rushing and "no time to lose" that sends us careening from one activity to another (mentally if not physically).

There is a significant difference between "moving fast" and "rushing." A lifelong teacher of these principles was once running on his way to a lecture. He had taught these techniques to thousands, and it so happened that one of his students was present and saw him running to a lecture for which he was late. The student said to him, "Oh, don't rush." Upon hearing this comment, the man whirled around and said, "You can run calmly or you can run nervously, but not to run when you are late is just irresponsible!" Then he ran off.

The point is well-taken. Speed in and of itself poses no problem. It is true, however, that, like driving a car, the faster we go the more difficult it becomes to steer well. In principle, there is nothing different required when driving quickly: the steering is about the same, all the car parts work about the same way, and the mirrors and windows are just as clear. But the speed makes it easier to miss something and demands more attention for us to drive well. This is also true in our lives where speed is fine if we know how to handle it. Otherwise we are like the inexperienced teenager rather than the trained race-car driver. Perhaps it may make sense to slow down a bit until we develop the skill to drive quickly, mistake-free, and in a non-agitated state.

We make choices in our lives that encourage us to feel both out of control and that there is a lack of sufficient time to do what we need to do. We eat breakfast, read the paper, and perhaps have the TV on all at the same time. We're on the phone, checking email, shaving, and half thinking about the kids all at the same time. We think we're saving time by piling things on, but in fact we are damaging our nervous systems and creating a decreased ability to concentrate. One can take amphetamines ("speed") to work faster, and the results are temporarily beneficial, but the long-term effect is extremely harmful. So too with overloading our nervous system without regard for its capabilities.

Instead, we need to train the mind to be able to handle what we pile on just as we'd need to train the body before lifting heavy weights. To omit the latter training leads to damaging the body, and likewise we damage the mind when we create an endless list of items we don't ever get to.

Try doing one thing at a time. Eat breakfast slowly and consciously, aware of each mouthful and of your chewing. Why not try it as an experiment? If you are *unable* to eat slowly and consciously, it may be a sign of overload and a lost ability to concentrate. One need not move slowly, but one ought to be able to move slowly without feeling anxious or restless. If this is not possible, the nervous system needs to be tuned up, if not overhauled.

Stop – Breath – Reflect – Choose

In *The Wellness Book* Dr. Herbert Benson and Eileen M. Stuart describe a four-step process they developed. This process is very helpful as it breaks into simple steps a method for choosing our response rather than merely reacting to circumstances. The four steps are: Stop – Breathe – Reflect – Choose. Let's go over each step carefully.

Stop – Almost all of our interpersonal difficulties arise because we don't stop. We tend to react to our circumstances immediately. Someone says something we don't like or agree with and – whoops – our response comes right out of our mouth without hesitation. It takes one moment to "speak our minds" and weeks to clean up the mess we have just created.

Our brains have a developed neocortex. That means we can be self-aware in a way that animals cannot. If you annoy a strange dog long enough, it will bite you. Dogs are not self-reflective. They can't think, "I'm going to bite him. But you know, he knows my owner and if I bite him, he'll tell him and I might not get fed, and boy, I really like food. But I bet I can find some food somewhere else if I need to. The heck with it, I'm going to take a chance and bite him anyway – CHOMP!" Dogs don't have the ability to stop and reflect on their actions. We do even if we often fail to exercise that ability.

Most of us have learned not to verbalize our judgmental or unpleasant thoughts. Certainly we have mostly learned not to "bite." But our judgmental and critical thoughts are still doing internal damage, even when we don't speak them. There is usually no pause between the stimulus and the automatic mental response. Unlike Fido, we can, with practice, train ourselves to stop before we react, physically, verbally, or mentally. The first step is to stop the physical/verbal action and then take that discipline inward.

There's a specific physical cue that you can use to help yourself to stop before acting. Sometimes we find ourselves in a situation where someone is saying something that we feel is inappropriate or not pertinent, whether in a personal situation or at work. You may notice a sensation of physical tension, almost pressure, in the chest. It's as if we're just waiting for him to pause and inhale for just a moment. That will give us the split second we need to interrupt him and stop his comment dead in its tracks.

If you are feeling that sensation in the chest, it's your clue you're experiencing stress. As soon as you feel that tightness and urge to speak, you know you are not thinking clearly because you are "on drugs." It is unlikely that a comment said while in that state is the very best thing to say. But if you take a step back instead and "watch the movie," you'd be very likely to know what to say.

Again, this is not about being passive. It is about clearing your own mind first before you act. Clear minds produce positive results. Minds feeling compulsion and tension born of desperation do not. I have worked to train myself so that whenever I'm with others and feel that tension in the chest, I immediately press my lips together. It's hard to speak in that pose! A good general rule would be: Never speak to relieve your own tension. Instead, release the tension – do a few rounds of the breathing exercises introduced in the meditation section of this book, or just "watch the movie" – and speak once your mind is clear.

Breathe – Every meditation technique works with the breath. The breath is closely related to heart rate, blood flow, and a host of physiological responses. Just taking a deep breath can change how the world looks to us. Right now, as an experiment, sit up straight, take a deep breath, tense all the muscles in your body for a few seconds vibrating the whole body slightly as you do it, and then throw your breath out strongly through the mouth, relaxing as you exhale. You will likely feel more awake and energized just from that one ten-second act. Various breathing techniques and their remarkably proven effects on the mind and body will be explored later.

Reflect – Here's where we take a step back and "watch the movie." As we have described earlier, we are looking at the scene with others in it and are not ourselves the lead characters. Once we are no longer personally and emotionally involved, we start to see things differently.

Using our very first example, we notice that the other person may be blind and we naturally feel compassion or understanding rather than judgment and annoyance. We may even come to see that it does not really matter whether he is blind, or even why he did what he did. Our job is how *we* respond and not to be the policeman or judicial appointee for others' behavior. Once we are free and clear-minded, there is no harm in looking at and evaluating the behavior of others, but our tendency is to want to do that first while we are still personally and emotionally involved. In that state – "on drugs" as we have called it – there are no good results either for us or for them.

Choose – Here's where we take control. Once we have done steps one through three, we are in a position to go to step four and make the right choice in both physical action and in attitude. "Choose" does not just refer to action, because stress (as we have defined it) is primarily a mental phenomenon. Our mental state is at least as important as our actions, and in fact, the mind always precedes behavior. Our actions always start as an idea or mental impression, so if we can control our minds, our actions will follow.

Simply repressing your feelings and behavior without changing perceptions will not work in the long run. Instead you can apply your energy to what you *are* able to control, which is yourself. As we have seen, stress is often primarily a function of feeling out of control. Yet given that there is an infinite number of things that we are not in control of, it cannot be dependent merely on lack of control. There are many things we cannot control that do not bother us. It also becomes a question of whether we think we are *supposed* to be in control of a particular thing

or circumstance. Making choices puts us back in the
driver's seat and leaves us feeling *in* control. It's just that
control needs to be directed at ourselves first rather than
the world around us.

Take Control of Your Inner Dialogue

Part of choosing is also altering what we might call our
"internal talk." All of us have an internal dialogue going
on most of the time. This chatter in our minds often
leaves us feeling either victims of the world around us,
angry at it, defeated by it, misunderstood by it, or in some
other unhelpful state. "Why did this have to happen to
me?" "How can he have done that to me after all I've
done for him?" "I failed again – I'll never get it right."
"I'm so (fill in your favorite pejorative), no wonder no
one can stand me."

If you had a friend that verbalized these things, you
would immediately say to your friend something like,
"Come on. You know that's not true. You're not perfect,
but neither are you nearly as bad as you're saying. You're
exaggerating this way out of proportion." Well, say that to
yourself! If it's true for your friend, why wouldn't it be
equally true for you?

Take a step back and look at that person in the movie.
We can reach a point where we are even impersonal with
ourselves. Sometimes when I make a mistake in a situation,
I think, "Well, I'm pretty sure I'll make at least another
5,000 more mistakes between now and the time I die. So
this was just one of them. Oh well." If I meet someone
who dislikes me, I may think, "There are six billion

people on this planet. Surely several hundred million of them would dislike me if they met me. So I guess I just ran into one. Big deal. Bound to happen someday." Stepping back works wonders to quiet the mind's negative patterns. Run the talk you would have if a friend of yours were discouraged rather than the talk that brings you down and leaves you feeling victimized and out of control. The world is not really happening to you or at you — it's just happening.

How to Choose Even When We Are Upset

Exercising choice does not mean repressing your feelings. A friend of mine who has been teaching these principles for a long time had quite a good opportunity to use them in the heat of battle. She was in Hawaii on vacation with her husband, and while there, they encountered a common married couple's dilemma. She wanted to buy gifts for people back home. He was all for the idea but didn't really want to deal with it and actually do the shopping. She had her list of all their friends and precisely who liked what, but he had put off their going into a gift shop until the last day, so by the time they got there she was already a little tense. They walked in and he looked around in a halfhearted way when suddenly he spied the answer to his prayers: a whole shelf of large plastic brown whistles that said "Aloha!" on them in Day-Glow green. He swept about twenty of them into a big shopping bag and announced cheerfully, "O.K. honey, we're done shopping. And I don't know what I was so concerned about. That whole process only took about two minutes!"

She was, let's say, "unimpressed"with his gift selection. But given her annoyance, and without denying that she was in fact annoyed, she was still able to step back and "watch the movie." Remember, no matter what we're feeling at any given moment, there is some range of options available to us. As long as we choose within the range of what is truly realistic for us at that moment, we're not denying what we really feel. Do not pretend to be feeling fine about something that you're upset about, but exercise choice given your current state of mind. Choose something that's within your actual range of realistic responses – but choose!

Her first thought was, "Should I vaporize him right here in the store? No, I can do better than that." Then she mentally moved to the other side of the spectrum. "Am I feeling perfect love and forgiveness? Heck no!" Then back the other way, though not quite as far. "Should I yell at him on the sidewalk? No, I think I can do better than that." Next, back again. "Can I manage never to talk about this again? No way. I'll die if I don't talk about this." She finally decided to talk to him when they got back to the hotel room. So even though the feelings were difficult and strong, she was still able to choose her response given her actual realistic range of possibilities.

When they got back to the hotel room, she put the "Do Not Disturb" sign on the outside of the door, deadbolted the door, and said, "We need to talk." And they talked about what had happened. What would have happened if she had blown up at him in the store? He'd have gotten defensive, she'd have gotten even angrier at his not "hearing her," and they never would have discussed what had occurred. (If you really want to get the other person personally and emotionally involved for some reason, try shouting at them. It works almost every time!) Instead they just talked about it, and each left feeling better and with understanding of what had happened between them.

She felt great because she had chosen her response and actually mastered herself in the situation. We always feel better when we're the one making the choice rather than simply reacting out of control.

Whom Can I Blame?

Now it may occur to you that our shopper in this story lost because she wound up getting stuck with those dumb whistles by waiting until they got back to the hotel. But the anger and frustration we so often feel is almost never about the "whistles" in our lives. It's more often related to something like "I've told you a million times this was important to me. You never listen or care about what I want." It is much better to address the underlying issue than just deal with the whistles, because next time it won't be whistles but something else. If the *process* is done right, the stress and communication is handled on a deeper level. Whistles do not cause stress. Needing the world (or spouse) to be different causes stress. If we practice what we have described here, not only is our stress greatly reduced, but our interpersonal relationships are very likely to take a big step forward as well. Once we have stepped back, we are a lot more likely to choose a response that will bear good fruit.

There seems to be a tremendous feeling of being a "victim" in the United States right now. Everyone feels that he or she is part of some group that is being exploited. And if someone doesn't know what group they are part of and how they are being taken advantage of, there are those who are anxious to educate them so that they can feel awful as soon as possible. Then, when things go wrong we can all look to assign blame somewhere and sue each other. This is not to say that there aren't injustices in this world that need to be corrected. But a society filled with "victims" is not one that can courageously and energetically tackle tough problems, because difficulties and challenges are always "someone else's fault." Some things actually *are* someone else's fault, but our first responsibility is to master our own reactive process, which will not only have us feel better than placing blame, but will also help us see where responsibility actually does lie. Once we are masters of ourselves, we will know both what to do and more importantly, whether to act at all. Just because something happens that you don't like doesn't mean it is someone's fault. Nor does it mean that it should change. Your not liking something is not the best standard by which to evaluate reality.

We can look at our lives as a series of free choices. Of course there are things that come up where we have no choice (like gravity), but we can instead focus on the areas where we do have free choice. Always affirm mentally to yourself, "I am a free person. I choose my response to whatever situation I face. If I can alter the situation to the good, I will do so with calm detachment. If not, I will do whatever I can to make the best out of that which cannot be changed." If you can practice and increasingly adopt this attitude, stress will no longer be a significant factor in your life.

We Choose What to Focus On

A friend of mine has been in a difficult situation for some time. He has a rare inoperable brain tumor. Given that surgery is not possible, he has undergone a series of radiation and chemical treatments that have left him with some impairments. He has always been a vibrant, hardworking, physical person. The treatments have resulted in nothing that an acquaintance can see, but they have taken some of his strength and abilities – enough that he can't do what he used to do. The doctors don't know whether this is a permanent condition or whether his abilities will come back.

Naturally, this has left him deeply frustrated and somewhat angry, as it would most people. When we were together, the subject turned to his situation. I said, "You know, you don't need to focus on what it is that you can no longer do. In fact, this situation has opened up some opportunities for you to do things you would never have been able to do, and may never have the chance to do again. You like to write. Here you are, off from work for the first time in your adult life, and unable to work with your horses as you've always loved to do. If you had all your physical stamina, you'd be out there right now with the horses. Instead you have this golden opportunity to do as much writing as you like. You may never be in this position again. It's almost as if every other door has been closed to you. Rather than hurling yourself at the doors that are now closed, why not joyfully go through the one that is still open? You've always wanted to write more. Now's your chance."

So many times and in so many ways it's as if there were a large white sheet in front of us with a black dot on it. We sometimes stand with our eye one inch from the black dot and claim the whole world is black. There are always white parts and black parts. Stepping back gives us the ability to see both. The black dot may be there, but focusing on it is not required. If we can *do* something about it, that's what we should do (Go get that tennis ball!) but staring at the black dot and then claiming everything in the world is black is neither helpful nor true.

Watching the Movie When in Crisis

A man once went through a trying health crisis. It was quite an experience for him, but was also instructive. I will share it as it was told to me:

> Many years ago, in the fall as I was just starting college, I had a mysterious illness. I would wake up each morning and feel sick to my stomach and unable to eat. I finally went to the local hospital. They administered a series of tests but were unable to find the cause. In the meantime my condition steadily worsened, and I soon left school and returned home to my parents.
>
> After another week or two my mother, who had become almost frantic at this point watching her son waste away, decided we would go to Florida where we had some fine medical contacts. We left early the next morning.
>
> When we arrived at the airport in Florida, my vision was blurred and I was immediately checked into the local hospital. By now the brain tumor that had been causing the problems was obvious, and I was prepped for immediate surgery. There was simply no time to lose.

After the successful surgery and a week or two of recovery, I woke up one morning with all the old symptoms. As you can imagine, this set the whole family into an emotional tailspin. Had they missed part of the tumor? Was damage done during the operation? Everything seemed to have been removed. What was causing the same symptoms as before? No one knew.

At one point the neurosurgeon came into my hospital room and said, "There have been some complications. We don't know exactly what is wrong, and we cannot operate again (today's modern scanning technology had not yet been invented). In fact, we don't know whether you will live until tomorrow. And if you do, we don't know about your making it to the next day. It will be day-to-day for at least a few weeks. The only thing we can do is wait to see what happens." I gulped and said, "O.K. Thanks for telling me." The doctor replied, "You didn't really understand what I said." I said, "Yes, I did." And repeated all the details back to him. At that point he sent in a psychiatrist, figuring I just wasn't relating to the reality of the situation.

The psychiatrist came in, and we talked for about forty-five minutes. Afterwards he spoke to the neurosurgeon and said, "He seems to understand the picture completely. He's just dealing with it very well. I'd leave him alone.

This experience turned out to be a formative one in the man's life. I know this for certain because I was that man! I remember clearly what happened when the doctor first told me what the situation was. This was the first time I had the experience of "watching the movie." I felt as if I were watching a movie of a man with complications after brain surgery, that the last reel had already been written, shot, edited, and printed, and that I would just have to wait and watch to see how it all turned out. It all felt entirely impersonal though it concerned my very life.

As it turned out, the complications passed on their own as the trauma of the tumor and surgery receded. Within a year I was back to my normal weight and health with no side effects from the ordeal.

After this experience was over I was struck at how calm I was throughout. I knew I had not been in "denial" nor unrealistic in my outlook about what might come, but that the ability to avoid becoming personally and emotionally involved with the melodrama had helped me get through it not only with concentration and awareness of what was happening, but also with a positive attitude. It was then that I realized that no matter what we face, our attitudes and perceptions have more effect on us than the circumstances themselves.

From this early experience I became deeply interested in the study of the human mind. Over time and through several twists and turns, this lifelong process of exploration and discovery has led me to the founding of Clarity Seminars and subsequently this book as a way to help others go through their own hard times, whether life-threatening or the less dramatic things we each face every day.

We Can Develop Confidence in Any Situation

Picture a martial artist walking down the street in a bad neighborhood at one a.m. on a Saturday. He may not be happy to be there, but he is surely less tense and nervous than I would be. What is his basic attitude? Self-confidence. That's because he knows that he can handle almost any situation he's likely to encounter. Of course, anything is possible, and someone could shoot him from a window. Despite that unfortunate possibility, his self-perception is, nonetheless, an attitude that he is ready for whatever might come.

Each of us can become martial artists of the mind. We can train ourselves to be able to mentally and emotionally handle whatever comes. We can become masters of Stop – Breathe – Reflect – Choose and feel in control of ourselves in almost any situation. We will still encounter 500 pound weights that we cannot lift, just as a black belt martial artist may face something he cannot defeat, but this needn't change our self-confidence any more than the fact that the martial artist could be shot from a window changes his.

Step Back and Still Respond Instantly

A common question at this point is, "O.K. I can see how Stop – Breathe – Reflect – Choose can enable me to make better choices, feel more in control, and reduce the reactivity all of which can reduce my level of stress. But things happen too fast. How can I start that process in everyday life in the heat of the moment?"

Perhaps an example or two will demonstrate how this can work, no matter what the circumstance. I play a little golf and remember the first time I went to a practice range with a more experienced golfer. She had kindly offered to show me how to swing the club, but to me it sounded like a hundred time-consuming instructions: "Hold the club like this, put these fingers here, put your head here, your left foot here, your right foot here, your elbows here, your . . ." I never knew I had so many body parts. Then came my favorite instruction: "Now relax and swing at the ball." I felt like if I even moved I'd fall over! But after a few weeks I started to get the hang of where everything went, and I could just pick up a club and go right into the proper stance (sometimes).

The same is true with Stop – Breathe – Reflect – Choose. At first our initial efforts may seem cumbersome and ponderous. But after a time they simply become who you are and how you look at the world. They become your automatic responses to circumstances.

Of course this takes practice. But when we consider the amount of time and energy we devote to our hobbies, our pastimes, and even to television and movies, what can be more rewarding than dedicating some time to improving our lives, our attitudes, and our entire outlook on life? (not to mention the time we'd save when we learn to stop worrying and regretting!) You may not become a "black-belt" in the art of stepping back, but if our goal is to move in the right direction, significant improvement is absolutely doable, if we devote even a little effort.

We can develop a virtually instant Stop – Breathe – Reflect – Choose response that simply becomes how we naturally respond to the world around us as second nature, just like that golf stance. Over time what seemed cumbersome and artificial simply becomes who we are. When 200-pound weights show up, we may find it quite difficult to engage this process, but we should not be discouraged. As we have said, the goal is directional improvement. If today you can only practice this on your two-pound weights, per-haps next month you will be able to do this on your ten-pound weights. And then twenty pounds after that.

Free From the Behavior of Others

I always enjoy hearing unusual victory stories from people who have been able to master something that had in the past been especially challenging for them. I'd like to share a situation where a woman was able, through real effort and determination, to lift a fairly large weight on her first try.

A woman who had previously attended our program came into the room quite excited. I asked her what was up and she related the following story:

> I have a teenage son at home, and one of his fa-vorite things to do is to bait me. He just loves to make me react by telling me things he knows will upset me. I think he likes to see my reactions take over. Well, I had just taken your class last week, and I knew when he'd be home that day, so I decided to prepare. I listened to a DVD of your talk for an hour and then practiced the half-hour meditation CD. When I finished, I felt like I was on top of the world. I was ready to meet the chal-lenge! Sure enough, he walked in soon after.
>
> The first thing he said to me was, "Gee, Mom, I wanted to tell you that I didn't get in until about one in the morning last night." This usually gets a rise from me as I have always asked him to be in by midnight. Instead, my reaction was to just look at him calmly and say, "Oh?" He seemed surprised but tried a second as-sault. He told me that, though he really had intended

to, he had forgotten to gas up the car and it was now on empty. He was again surprised when I responded with an even-minded, "Oh really?" He paused for a few moments and looking right at me said, "Gosh, Mom, what's gotten into you? I'm really impressed." We then had the best talk we've had since he became a teenager. We talked for about forty-five minutes about everything under the sun. I'm sure that happened because I had broken the cycle of reacting, and we could see each other as people rather than as buttons to push and be pushed by. My automatic out-of-control reactive responses were over.

I asked her how she felt about this turn of events, and she said she felt like a million dollars, as if a great weight had been taken off her back. She also said that she felt that practicing this as much as possible will make her a much better parent. Rather than reacting out of control when her son behaves inappropriately, she can now see what is best and make that choice. In the past she would react to him, he would react to her reaction, and it would just deteriorate from there. Remember, the chance of our emotional reaction resulting in our doing the best thing in a difficult situation like that is about zero. If we really take a step back, reflect on what's happening, and make our best choice, we are almost sure to make the right one.

Freeing the Mind, Not Memorizing Tips

People often ask me what they should do in a given situation. I've always been hesitant to address specific situations for two reasons.

First, they know the situation better than I. They know the people involved, themselves, the background conditions, etc. My goal is not to tell them what to do or say but to clear their minds in order to create a mind-set so that *they* know what the right thing is to do. By helping them to take a step back and remove their feeling of being personally and emotionally involved, they can usually come up with a good next step.

Secondly, it is the deep habit of the mind to want to change the circumstance rather than changing its own habits and attitudes. The goal of this system is to change our attitudes and mentally destructive habits, not to get the husband to go shopping or the son to behave. Even though we feel that it's those things that are causing our stress, they are not, and addressing those circumstances is only the most temporary of fixes. The next day there will be something else amiss that upsets us, and something else the day after that. To be able to master Stop – Breathe – Reflect – Choose is to find the key to the jailhouse door. Once that key is firmly in our possession, no bars can hold us.

Once we are mentally free, we can then try whatever idea we like. We can still get the situation to work out, but we are doing it *after* we have stepped back and are free from stress. Not before. Focusing on our inner state before addressing the difficult circumstance enables us to reduce our stress by developing a sense of control, while not eliminating any option in dealing with the circumstance. This approach is the best of both worlds.

VIII

HOW MUCH DO WE REALLY KNOW?

Another obstacle that seems to prevent us from taking a step back is a more subtle one. We seem to feel and act as if we know everything about any given situation. Though absurd, we constantly make assumptions and jump to conclusions. What is more strange is that we often assume things that leave us feeling terrible!

Remember the man who bumped us on the bus? We felt better when we turned around and saw that he was blind. We could have just assumed he was blind when we got bumped. We certainly didn't know one way or the other. In fact, the question of whether he was blind or not is not any of our business. People rarely behave in a random manner. People do what they do for a reason, no matter how ridiculous or inappropriate that reason seems to us. We may not see what led up to their behavior. We may not see what particular delusion or blindness of theirs caused them to behave as they did. We may not know how they were brought up, what awful event recently happened to them, or anything else. But why does any of that matter? Our job is *our* response, not their behavior. This does not let them off the hook if what they did was wrong, but it gets us started looking at the only thing we can truly influence: ourselves. Why focus on them first when we ourselves have work to do?

We Rush to Judgment

We go through our entire day making judgments and reacting as if we always know the whole picture. In fact, we virtually never know the whole picture and usually know just a small portion of what's relevant to the situation we're facing.

Suppose you were walking down the street and saw a man hit a cute little dog in the back. You'd likely think he was awful and cruel. What if you then found out that the dog had had a bone stuck in its throat, and the slap was to help dislodge the bone? You'd then think the man was a hero. But suppose you then found out that he didn't know about the bone when he hit it? Now you'd think, "I knew he was cruel in the first place. I could just tell." But *then* you found out. . . . We can play this game forever. The fact is we move back and forth with our judgments and grievances at lightning speed as new data is presented, each time feeling sure that we are justified in our feelings.

Wouldn't it be better to just accept that there is more going on around us than meets the eye, and that we almost always just have a piece of the puzzle? After all, what is gained by being so certain of the opinions we have? When confronted with a disturbing situation, we can mentally step back and think, "That's interesting. I wonder what is going on? That's certainly not how I would have dealt with it." The act of even considering that there are circumstances we may not be aware of lessens our commitment to being personally and emotionally involved. One can even make a bit of a game of it, seeing if there is an explanation for what happened that upset us, rather than assuming the other person is of poor character and "had no right to. . . ." He may, or may not have had a right to do what he did, but what about *your* reaction? Are you free right now? You can deal with his behavior later. Your first priority is to become inwardly free yourself.

This is not to say that we seek to become so open-minded that our brains fall out! There's a big difference between an open mind and an empty mind. What we are striving for is to become genuinely interested and involved observers of the world around us. We see what happens, practice Stop – Breathe – Reflect – and Choose, and we make a response based on everything we know and everything we consider. Such an approach is an antidote for stress, a guarantee that we are doing the best we can, and a recipe for leading a happier more productive life. We come to feel in control of ourselves rather than victims of circumstance in a harsh world.

Practicing in Life's Hardest Situations

Sometimes people say that this is all well and good for dealing with the ten-pound weights, but what about when something really *hard* shows up? Let's look at perhaps the most dramatically awful situation one can imagine – being thrust into a concentration camp like those of World War II. What could possibly be worse than to suffer such a fate?

Most who went through that horror were killed or psychologically scarred in some way from their experience. But I have read the autobiographies of several people who not only managed to survive the awful experiences but actually grew stronger and came to shine through them. They all seemed to have one attitude in common: "You can humiliate me, you can break my bones, you can even kill me, but my mind and heart are mine, and there's nothing you can ever do about it." Those brave people were free in a most important way even amidst their bondage. For the most destructive bondage we face is one of our own making. It is the prison of our minds. To free the mind is to end suffering and sorrow, even in the middle of the most difficult of circumstances. If this can be done in a concentration camp, as these people have shown, it can be done in whatever situation we may face.

Experiences like these show us why it is a huge advantage to start practicing here and now and not later. We make things much more difficult if we wait until a 300-pound weight shows up in our lives, take this book out, give it a quick read, and then try to implement its ideas. We're working with habits of reacting that have built up over many years. It will take patience, practice, and effort to change them. The good news is that directional change happens almost instantly if we really try what we've been discussing, but we need to start now, not later, if we wish to make substantial progress.

How Does a Bad Day Start?

Let's hope this doesn't happen to you, but some days just get off on the wrong foot. You wake up and see your alarm clock didn't go off, and your first mental reaction is "Oh no!" Then you burn your toast. "Oh no!" Then you break your shoelace. "Oh no!" Then you drop your newspaper in a puddle. Then your car won't start. Then you hit every red light. Then you can't find parking. Then you don't have your passkey to get into the building. Then you have twenty voice mails and thirty-seven emails. Then you realize you forgot your early-morning meeting. Then. . . .

At each step of the way there is a part of you that complains mentally about the "movie." You finally get to your desk, it's not even 9 a.m., and you've already yelled at the movie fifty-three times! No wonder you feel stress. Every time we yell at the movie we are reinforcing the idea that circumstances control our lives, the idea that we are completely dependent on external conditions for our happiness and well-being.

Suppose you just bought a pen yesterday. You're at your desk and it breaks in half. You think, "Hey! I just bought this pen yesterday. What's going on here?" You then grab another and think no more of it. What you may not realize is that a ninety-nine cent piece of plastic just controlled you. Your mood was altered because of its behavior.

Now, one instance of this means little in itself, but multiply this incident by 500,000 times a year and we have a problem. Just as Gulliver was held down by the thousands of threads the tiny Lilliputians wove around him, we are bound and feel thwarted by our countless desires and preferences. Each little thought of "victim" or "it's making me feel . . ." binds us and weakens us. Eventually there are so many threads we feel overwhelmed, unable to move even an inch. We are bound by our own sense of being set upon by an unfair and uncaring world. Each individual little item means nothing, but when we add millions of them together over the years, they weave a web of confusion and a sense of defeat that binds as tightly as any steel ever could. We are in bondage to the dictatorship of our own minds.

King of the Universe

One evening I was at a hall about to give a public lecture. We had done a corporate training program that same afternoon, so my day had been tightly scheduled. Everything was going smoothly, except that I had forgotten to eat! Fortunately, there was a snack bar with a deli area in the hall, so I went up to order a simple sandwich. I was in a bit of a rush as I placed my order.

The fellow behind the counter treated every aspect of making this sandwich as if it were delicate surgery. First he took out the loaf of bread. He started to untwist the twist-tie on the bag. One twist. Two twists. Three twists, each done deliberately and carefully. At last! The tie was loose. He removed a piece of bread. Studied it (perhaps to ascertain that it was a true rectangle), placed it on the counter, and reached into the bag for its mate. It, too, proved to be rectangular. Now it was time to reach for the cheese. All the while I am thinking, "Just great. I am experiencing the world's first three-hour sandwich. I hope he's done sometime this evening."

Then suddenly an image flashed into my mind. In my mind's eye I was in kingly robes waiting for that sandwich. I was surprised at the image and filed the thought for later as it had piqued my curiosity. Eventually I realized what it was all about. That was David Gamow, Lord of the Universe. I was about to deliver justice to the man behind the counter: "Off with his head for impeding my progress," I would bellow.

My view of the matter was that somehow he was offending my royal personage and, as the center (justifiably, I might add!) of the Universe, something very wrong was happening. In fact, all that was really happening was that someone was making a sandwich slowly. Even though we know better, we somehow feel that everything should revolve around us and are distressed when things don't conform to that idea.

Did They Really Arrange to Get In Front of Us?

Sometimes we drive to get to the highway, proceed on the exit ramp, turn the last corner, and see a sea of red taillights. Upon seeing the endless traffic, as we have seen, most of us react with stress in such a situation. But there is an interesting undercurrent that contributes to the distress. I suspect that most people feel as if somehow all those other motorists must have called each other and agreed to get on the highway ahead of us just to slow us down. Doesn't it feel like there's some sort of a plot afoot? "Why me?" is being asked in hundreds of cars simultaneously as if each car were having a unique experience.

As we have already seen, we tend to become personally and emotionally involved with things that happen around us. Of course, sometimes people do actually direct things personally at you. But even in those cases we can step back and realize that they are just being the way they are and that our response to their behavior is still up to us. Situations where the other person really intends to hurt us are harder to master, so let's not start with those 100-pound weights.

The traffic example makes it clear that even in situations where nothing at all "personal" is going on, we still easily slip into the old harmful attitudes. If we start practicing with situations where it is clearly just the world unfolding in a way we happen not to like, we will begin the process of mastering ourselves and will soon see that, with further practice, we can apply these techniques even when it *is* personal.

Though we are often consumed with a situation's effect on us, our part is often quite small when seen from a larger perspective. I read a quote once that stimulated much thought: "I am merely a bit player in my postal carrier's melodrama." From my postal carrier's perspective I am but one passing minor character. There is much more going on around here than just us! Seeing the whole picture prevents us from envisioning ourselves as the center of the universe, a good start at stepping back.

IX

MATURITY

I once heard a very interesting and powerful definition of maturity, and it has stuck with me ever since: maturity can be defined as "the ability to relate to other people's realities as well as we relate to our own." We have all met people like this. They are centered in themselves and seem at home with everyone and in all circumstances. They seem to be understanding and to have a knack for getting along with others. They also seem to draw the best out of the people around them. I believe that these abilities are a result of maturity as defined above. The more mature the individual, the more he is able to see the world through the eyes of others. Don't we all appreciate people who seem to understand and accept us? Don't they also seem generally to be happier and more content within themselves? It is not because they are shut down or unaware of the troubles of the world. It is because they have learned to master their own reactive process. They are no longer personally and emotionally involved with everything that happens around them.

A baby is completely immature, and thus is unable to relate to the world beyond itself. From a baby's perspective, the entire universe revolves around it and its wants and needs. An adult who is truly mature can see others' points of view easily. That's not to say that he would necessarily agree with them, but that he can relate to them and understand them as if he had seen their perspective through their own eyes. The compassion and understanding that naturally result from this seeing-through-their-eyes ability are wonderful antidotes to stress.

Another interesting way to view this can be seen when we notice a fundamental rule of the human mind and emotions. It can be simply stated this way: "The more we think of ourselves, the less happy we are." Maturity, compassion, and true selfless service require us, by their very nature, to shift the focus away from ourselves. These attitudes are about other people, not ourselves, and thus require us to relinquish the lead role in the movie. It is for this reason that helping others always leaves us feeling better.

We Are Happiest When Thinking of Others

The principal idea is that we are happy when we think of others and less so when we are focused on ourselves. Stress is only possible when we want the world to be *our* way, and thus is necessarily related to thinking about ourselves, our needs, and our desires.

People who are very depressed have a difficult time expanding past their own small world. The covers are pulled over their heads, the lights are dimmed, and, the curtains are drawn closed. They have collapsed inward and cannot see beyond their own pain. This is not a criticism but is just a simple statement of what has happened to their consciousness. While in this condition, relating to the reality of others is almost impossible.

People who spend much of their time serving others, however, tend to be more joyful. Their perspective is expansive. I had the great fortune of spending a short time with Mother Teresa many years ago. She was a tiny woman, but her energy and joy filled the whole room. She was radiant, though quite elderly at the time. She also was known for not thinking about herself, and even near death she was primarily concerned about the good of her Order.

We are happy in exact inverse proportion to how involved with ourselves we are. Unfortunately, some people who serve others do so for their own more self-oriented reasons: to look good, assuage guilt, or other motives that are simply disguised "thinking about themselves."

It's ironic that the phrase "looking out for No. 1," which is intended as a philosophy to ensure you get what you need to be happy, is actually a recipe for just the opposite. Such people are always worried that they will not get what they feel is due them, or worried that someone will take what they already have and have worked so hard to get. They multiply the ways in which they need the world to be their way, and thus multiply the number of things to watch out for, worry about, and feel threatened by. This attitude is a guaranteed stress inducer.

If your joy comes from power, you fear you may lose it; if your joy comes from money, that too needs protection; if your joy comes from health, an illness or accident can easily reverse that. But if your joy comes from deep inside, as those few concentration camp victims found, nothing can take it or threaten it. Focusing on what we have lost or might lose does not help us.

"What Might Have Been . . ."

A woman once approached me after a class. She was very distressed. As we spoke, I learned that she had had options in the stock of the technology company where we were speaking. In 1998, like many of the tech stocks, her stock began a dramatic rally. When the stock got to $145 a share in 2000, her husband begged her to sell it. She refused. Then when it dropped to $125, she said, "When it gets back to $145, I'll sell." Of course, it then went to $100. Then she decided she'd sell if it got back to $125. Unfortunately, by the time we spoke it had fallen to $7 a share and her options were now worthless. She said that she had had her dream in the palm of her hands – retiring, buying a home elsewhere, everything she wanted. She was so distraught at having messed up that she was now having trouble sleeping at night.

I asked how her husband was dealing with the situation, and she said he was fine with it, but that she could never forgive herself for what had happened. I pointed out that she was happy in 1998 before the stock's rise and that now in 2002, she was now in exactly the same position she was then. The only thing that had changed was her expectation and hopes and her regret at having made a mistake. But that point and everything else I said were of no comfort. She had tears in her eyes as we parted. Her external circumstances had not changed a bit in four years. She had not expected the rise when it started, nor had she planned on an early retirement. But once she had come to expect those things, her loss was devastating to her. What could be a clearer example of how our minds create our pain.

I did not point out to her that had she sold the stock right at its high, some other fate might have befallen her leading her into regret just the same. When we rely on our circumstances to bring us peace and joy, we are building our hopes on a foundation of sand. Only self-mastery can bring us the happiness we want.

Serve the Person Who Bedevils You

Sometimes it takes what initially sounds like extreme measures to broaden our perspective beyond our own needs and wants.

A woman once approached me right after a program. She was distressed because she was soon going to face a situation that she was feeling very tense and anxious about: spending five days visiting her mother-in-law. They had never gotten along. Whenever they were together, the mother-in-law would be sarcastic and make it clear that she never approved of her marriage in the first place. The situation was very hurtful, and the woman always hated her trips there. They would wind up sniping at each other for the whole week, and by the time she finally got home she was a wreck. She was sure that she wouldn't be able to practice Stop – Breathe – Reflect – Choose.

After listening to her story I made a suggestion that startled her. I suggested that no matter what happens, she should do whatever she could to *serve* her mother-in-law! I said, "Whatever else happens, always mentally ask the question, 'What can I do for her right now?' As if she were some celebrity you loved who was just passing through for a visit. It doesn't matter what else happens so long as you hold this one attitude. You don't have to like her. You don't have to respect her. You just have to serve her needs and wants. It doesn't need to be extreme (you don't need to lay your coat over a puddle), just reasonable and consistent, *as if* you really cared about her and her welfare."

She gulped hard and said she would try. As appalling as this suggestion was to her, it was about physical behavior only and thus seemed at least possible. She did not believe she could even get to "stop" in Stop – Breathe – Reflect – Choose because she was sure that her anger would overwhelm her right at the start.

I saw her about ten days later at a follow-up seminar. She was glowing and so excited she couldn't wait to tell me what had happened: "I did what you suggested, and it was initially incredibly hard and seemed to make no difference. On top of everything, I resented needing to be kind to her. At first my mother-in-law was just as rude as always. But after just a few hours things started to change. Serving her got easier and more natural, and she started to soften up! I couldn't believe it. And as I kept serving, she became kinder. This pattern continued until the end of the trip when she gave me the warmest hug I have every received from her as she thanked me for everything. It seemed like a miracle, and I couldn't wait to tell you."

This worked for two reasons. First, since the daughter-in-law never had time to think about herself when they were together, she felt less oppressed. We can only feel bad when thinking of ourselves. She had no time for that since she was always thinking about her mother-in-law's needs, rather than "How could she say that to me?" and "She has no right to treat me that way."

The second reason it worked was that the mother-in-law started saying "thank you." Of course, at first she just grunted when a kindness was shown to her, but after a time the dripping water of kindness wore through her stone heart. Once the "thank yous" started coming things really changed. It is very hard to keep sniping at someone you keep thanking! Slowly the mother-in-law convinced herself, by her own words, that the woman was perhaps not so bad after all.

We do not generally appreciate how our behavior and thoughts affect those around us. There is every likelihood that the mother-in-law could feel the woman's judgments of her even though the daughter-in-law was "sure" that she had previously "done nothing." When she followed the suggestion to serve her and constantly consider what she might need, she neutralized whatever judgments there may have been. Not at first, but after a short while her own attitude changed. The best antidote in such situations is a genuine change of perspective, which removes the judgmental thoughts at their root.

"Good Stress" vs. Bad Stress

You may wonder, "Isn't there such a thing as good stress?" The short answer is, "No. There isn't." It's true that we can use stress to enable us to do things we might not have done otherwise, but that does not make it good.

Suppose you need to get a large amount of work done in a short amount of time, and you are very tired. You could take amphetamines (speed) to stimulate yourself in order to get the job done. This "solution" has an enormous cost, however. It may give you a short-term burst of energy, but it in fact destroys you over time and ultimately reduces your ability to work at all, not to speak of the damage it causes your overall health and mind. Stress takes longer to do its damage, but studies consistently show how stress impairs mental abilities, rather than enhances them.

A much better solution is to learn how to accomplish what we need to do while maintaining control of ourselves. You may think that if someone were chasing you with a knife, you'd run faster, but this is only because it increases your motivation. It is far superior to motivate ourselves without stress. When running without stress, we can run even faster. Once we learn to have the right attitude, stress becomes unnecessary as a driving force and merely hampers our performance. Great athletes have all the adrenaline and energy they need when they need it without using stress, anxiety, fear, and worry to propel them forward. If you enjoy stress, you are enjoying the drug that gives you a high before the crash.

Some People Go From One Crisis to Another

Have you ever noticed that some people are always in a tizzy about something? From their perspective, there is

always something going on that is disturbing or unset-
tling. They seem to attract chaos and emotional turmoil,
or if not actually attract it, bring things to a boil whenever
they have the chance.

I was once at a holiday meal with a group of friends. It
was before the meal, and we were gathered in the living
room eating hors d'oeuvres. Suddenly, from the kitchen,
I heard a shout from the hostess. It sounded as if someone
were breaking in through the kitchen window to pillage
the house. I went running in to see what was happening.
The disaster that had prompted the shout was an inex-
pensive fork stuck in the garbage disposal! All that
emotion over such a minor event. How is one to find
peace with an approach to life like that?

There are so many things that can go wrong in our
everyday circumstances, if a little thing like a stuck fork
can create such unhappiness, what are we to do with the
thousands of other disappointments and travails that we
find ourselves in, some of which are of actual consequence? The only answer is to become more emotionally
independent of our circumstances.

Certain people seem always to be calm and flowing
with life's inevitable ups and downs. Surely some people
do have more difficulties in life than others. The mark of
a centered and stable person, however, is not what comes
to him but how he *responds* to what comes to him. That is
why we are always inspired by people who face adversity
with courage and optimism. It is not that they are
Pollyannas, or that they don't know fear, or don't grasp
what is happening. In fact, people who are too naïve to
relate to or understand difficulties or danger don't inspire
us but instead earn only a shake of the head and perhaps

a slight smile. It is those who are well aware of what they face but are able to rise above it and triumph that truly can be called great. Rather than dissolving in a puddle of "Woe is me" and "It's not fair," they pick themselves up and ask, "How can I respond to this?"

Not Unaware or Uncaring

This is not to say that we become unaware or uncaring, as this account that was related to me shows:

> I am a heart surgeon. I care passionately about my work and the people whose lives I touch. Yet it's essential for me to keep a certain emotional distance from what I do because I so often have someone's life in my hands. If I were to allow myself to become emotionally entangled with my patients, I would not be able to perform the surgery as well as I know I can. I know other doctors who seem to have more trouble with this and tend to get a little personally involved in some situations. When they do, I believe it hurts both their work and themselves. In a funny way, keeping that emotional detachment enables me to care more because the risk of becoming too involved is not there.

As we saw when we shared the example of helping the stranger on the street move the box, the more personally and emotionally involved we are the more we are thinking about ourselves.

I have often worked with nurses. As a group they are as caring, selfless, and giving as you will find. When working with them, I can often tell which particular new nurses are most likely to burn out from the job: They are the ones who *need* their patients to recover. Patients die. If a nurse needs her patients to recover to feel satisfied with her work, she will suffer. The ones who can avoid becoming emotionally involved do not care less. In fact, in many ways they are able to care more because they are not thinking of themselves and their own needs, only the needs of the patient and the situation.

I know when I speak to someone who is having a hard time and is seeking advice, it is important for me to avoid becoming personally and emotionally involved with his problem. If I do come to a point where I need him to hear me or see my point, I suddenly am no longer thinking about him or his needs, but am instead reacting to my own desires or discomfort. It starts with a good motive – wanting to help – but the result is always the same: an actual decrease in my ability to help. I wind up doing what I need to do to resolve my own discomfort, at least in part. For me to be able to sensitively tune into what needs to be said, I must become aware of what they need to hear. I cannot know what they need to hear when I am experiencing my own needs, which are sometimes in conflict with those of a client. The best way to counsel someone else is to learn how to put yourself aside as much as possible.

Selfless Service and True Advice

The highest form of service is, after all, selfless service where we are truly acting out of service and not for what we can get out of it. There are many times we "serve" while a large part of us is focused on how good it makes us look, how it makes us feel better about ourselves, or how it eases our discomfort. In fact there are usually several motives for each action, but we can try to limit self-preoccupation while enhancing true selflessness. If this seems like a suggestion to become self-denying or a martyr, it is not. Dynamic service will strengthen both your self-image and willpower, not weaken it. History is filled with countless examples of enthusiastic self-sacrifice leading to ever more courage and strength.

Service that is not truly selfless is like advice given by someone who says, "This is for your own good," while we know what he really means is, "I hate it when you do that!" Who is that advice really for? The recipient is much less appreciative because he knows the advice-giver is really just saying it for his own benefit. On the other hand, when someone gives advice that is based on genuine caring for us and our situation, we appreciate the effort even if the advice happens to be off the mark. This shows that it is not the advice itself, but the motivation behind the advice, that results in our gratitude or scorn for what was offered.

This is another example of how putting ourselves aside is appreciated and inspiring, whereas "what's in it for me" wins gratitude and admiration from no one, not even from ourselves.

X

"I DON'T WANT TO BE
THAT GOOD"

O ne of my friends, a very gifted teacher of these
principles, relates an interesting and instructive
story of an exchange he had with his own son.

> My nine-year-old came home from school having
> been bullied by another child. He was quite upset, and
> I comforted him as best I could. After a time when he
> had calmed down, I approached him again and started
> to chat with him in a quiet voice. I pointed out that the
> bully had some very difficult life circumstances and
> was probably quite unhappy. He may have been lash-
> ing out due to his deep and long-standing sense of
> helplessness and frustration. I further pointed out that
> what he probably needs more than anything is love
> and support from those around him, and how unfortu-
> nate it is that his behavior winds up drawing just the
> opposite response. After letting that all sink in I sug-
> gested that maybe my son could show him the
> kindness that has been so lacking in his life. He became

very quiet and thoughtful. After a little while he looked at me and spoke. "Daddy, I don't think I want to be that good a boy yet."

We smile at that story because it is so insightful and honest, and cuts a little close to home. Each of us has that part of us, though we may have learned enough by now not to verbalize it. Over time we come to see, however, that we are the ones who win when we become "that good of a boy" because the frustration we feel is rooted in holding on to the thought that the other person is the enemy.

Forgiveness

Stepping back and seeing the other person without personal involvement is also the best way to bring about forgiveness. A number of studies have shown that an inability to forgive is correlated with increased rates of heart attack, as well as a host of other maladies.

Psychologist Charlotte van Oyen Witvliet at Hope College in Holland, Michigan, asked seventy-one college students to think about someone who had hurt them and focus on the anger they felt toward that person. The subjects were wired with electrodes that measured how their bodies responded. While the students were nursing their grudges, their blood pressure surged and their heart rates increased. Their muscles tensed, and they perspired more. They were then asked to think about forgiving the offenders. The subjects' cardiovascular systems and nerves immediately calmed down. Dr. Witvliet commented that this is about "freeing yourself from the shackles of rage and resentment" not about becoming a doormat. The anger we feel is hurting us, not the object of our anger.

And this perspective from Stanford University:

> Studies show that forgiveness is not about absolving the perpetrator; it is about healing the victim. "Forgiveness isn't giving in to another person, it's getting free of that person,"*

Compromise

The idea of "giving up" or "becoming a doormat" is related to the defeat we can sometimes feel when we are "forced" to compromise. Feeling as though compromise is a defeat is only possible when we are not seeing and accepting reality for what it is. If we wanted our six-year-old to pick something up off the shelf when we were grocery shopping with him, we would not feel we were "compromising" if we acknowledged that he might be unable to pick up something very heavy and allowed him to lift something lighter instead. Fully taking reality into account is not compromising. We see his limitations and adjust our expectations accordingly.

We may see clearly that pushing our point and ignoring someone else's limitations will leave hurt feelings and so decide to back off. If so, we are not "giving in" but are simply acknowledging that the best overall course of action is to avoid hurting others. We feel defeated because

*Frederic Luskin, Director, Stanford Forgiveness Project, with Carl Thoresen, Professor of Education, Psychology, and Psychiatry at Stanford University.

we wish they could really hear what we have to say, but that is just wanting the world to be different to match our own ideas.

If we can show them that our idea really is best for them too, then we are free to try to do so. But if they are simply not going to see it, we must accept the world for the way it is and overcome the thought that they "should see my point." If they cannot because of some internal blindness, we must accept that each of us is blind in some way or another, and we have simply run into their blind spot. The only thing we are giving up is our desire for the world to be the way we want it to be rather than the way it is. We wish they would be different, but wishing does not make it so.

Finding Out What Ails Us Makes Us Feel Better

Have you ever been moderately sick and not known exactly what was wrong? Once you found out what was wrong, you "felt" better even though your medical condition was completely unchanged by the knowledge. The same is true with stress in our lives. Many people with whom I have worked over the years have found that deeply understanding the cause of their feelings was remarkably helpful. Often they would respond with a comment such as, "Oh, *now* I see what's going on!" This awareness in and of itself would be accompanied by a marked decrease in stress and concern. Seeing what happens to our minds as "the physics of how the mind works," rather than the world trying to "get us," brings tremendous relief.

Knowledge is also power. Once we come to see our stress response is internal and gain mastery over our reactive process, feelings of stress will begin to diminish significantly. This change of perception is radical and has deep and far-reaching effects. As hard as it may sound to do, it is much easier to change a step in a series of internal perceptions and chemical reactions than it is to persuade the universe to treat us differently!

What's Trying to Happen Here?

Another good trigger device that may enable us to step back from a situation is to mentally ask ourselves the simple question: "What's trying to happen here." Every word of this question has been carefully chosen. It is not, "What is happening to me here?" because we are taking the focus away from "me." It is asking, "What does the flow of the events seem to indicate is naturally unfolding?"

Asking this question causes us instantly to become less personally and emotionally involved. It is as though we are watching a movie and trying to see what the next plot development might be. Even if we are unable to answer the question, the mere act of stepping back to ask it is calming to the mind. Don't forget, if we are unable to answer the question, it's a sign that we are still too personally and emotionally involved and are starting with too heavy a weight. If you really step back mentally, you'll know "what's trying to happen here."

A second beneficial aspect of this question is that once it has removed you from the scene, it focuses on the needs of others. After asking, "What's trying to happen here," we may become aware of factors like, "Oh, I see. He's exhausted after a long day's work." Or, "Oh, it must be that she's just had an argument with her boss." As we tune into the people around us, we become both more compassionate and more understanding. These feelings are simply incompatible with stress. The next time you are facing a difficult situation, especially if it involves others (as it usually does), step back for a moment and ask, "What's trying to happen here?" and watch how your perspective instantly changes.

Upon stepping back we may not see the other person as justified in his behavior. In that case we can simply note that fact without attaching any value to it. We can think, "They really have a lot to learn about how to treat others" without anger, resentment, or hurt. We have simply observed a true state of affairs: their poor behavior. They are not more ill-mannered just because their rude behavior happened to be directed at us. There are two things going on: Their behavior and our reaction to their behavior. Our reaction is our responsibility not theirs. Noticing that they could have, in fact, acted better does not remove our responsibility from our own shoulders. And the more time we spend "evaluating" their behavior the less time we spend noticing our own, and the more likely we are to slip into judgment. Their behavior and motivations are really scarcely our business. Ours, however, are.

What's Trying To Happen Here – A Personal Experience

A number of years ago I was a keynote speaker at a conference in San Diego. My part had finished, and I was about to head home. When I called the airline, I found out that my flight had been canceled with the next available flight many hours later.

I had quite a bit of work waiting back at the office, so I put considerable effort into trying to get a flight out sooner, but my attempts got me nowhere. I was just beginning to get frustrated when finally, I stepped back and asked, "O.K. What's trying to happen here?" Suddenly it opened my mind to more possibilities than I had been considering. "Gosh, maybe I'm supposed to stay for a while." I booked the earliest flight I could and settled myself in the hotel conference area. The ski slope suddenly went to the left so rather than insisting on my game plan of turning to the right, I leaned to the left and I wondered with enthusiastic anticipation what would happen next. As it turned out, I made some important business contacts between the other sessions that were still going on. And the work waiting for me all got done in time anyway. Not only was my "need" to get back early mostly my own invention, but something much more important was trying to happen. I would have derailed those opportunities had I sat around sulking about my late return and not been wholeheartedly with the people I wound up meeting. And even if those opportunities had not turned up, I was certainly happier letting go of the canceled flight and moving on to whatever was next. It's not like our sulking actually ever helps the situation! If it did, we could at least argue that perhaps it's worth it to sulk (or worry, or complain). But in fact these attitudes actually prevent other positive things from happening, so we lose twice – once because the event we are upset about occurred and then a second time as we suffer for it far past the event itself.

Bus in Pakistan

A friend who has spent many years in India related a very funny and instructive story to me about an incident that occurred in neighboring Pakistan:

> A large bus had become stuck in the mud. The fifty or so people on board piled out to push the bus out. Everyone was pushing and groaning with the strain. The driver thought it seemed a bit strange to be taking so long, as it was just a small bit of mud and there were many people pushing. After a time he stepped back to survey the whole scene and burst out laughing. Half the people were pushing on one end of the bus and the other half just as hard on the other end!

This is, unfortunately, all too descriptive of what happens in our own minds. There are parts of us that really want something and other parts that are afraid of that very thing. Parts of us worry about what others will think. Other parts encourage us to proceed regardless of the opinions of others. Still other parts of us would rather just go out to dinner and forget the whole idea.

It's as if our own minds were populated by vastly different "mental citizens." There's the one who is always grumpy, the one who is always defeatist, the one who worries too much, and the lazy one. They are all there along with many others, each one representing a different mood or aspect of our personality, just as different types of people surround us in our daily lives. Each of us is a very complex combination of all of these qualities. If we could only get more of these mental citizens to cooperate with each other and push in the same direction, how much more effective we would be in everything we undertook!

The thwarting crosscurrents of our conflicting desires set us back in our otherwise sincere efforts just as much as those people pushing on both ends of the bus at the same time. What would happen if we could get all of our mental citizens pushing or pulling in the same direction?

The Law of Magnetism

If you were to examine a magnet on the molecular level, you'd see billions of molecules. Each individual molecule has a north-south polarity to it, just like the magnet itself. What gives a magnet its unusual attractive properties, unlike a normal object, is that each molecule is pointed the same way. That is, all the north-south poles are aligned. In fact, one can take an ordinary piece of steel and stroke it with a magnet (each stroke carefully in the same direction) and turn that piece of steel into a magnet. What you will have done is to induce the molecules in the piece of steel to align.

Another way to magnetize a bar of steel is by passing an electric current around it. This creates an electromagnet by aligning its molecules as well. We can perform an analogous process on ourselves! By passing a lot of energy through us (in the form of intention and willpower – much safer than using an electrical current!) we become much more "magnetic" as we align all of our thoughts and intentions in the same direction.

Lining up the "molecules" of our intentions and aspirations with our actions and behaviors brings personal magnetism and results in a steady gaze, firm stride, calm demeanor, and a purposefulness that is inspiring to others and deeply satisfying to ourselves as well. We all know or have seen people like this. They never seem to be off-balance. Regardless of what they are facing, they do not complain or bemoan their fate. It is difficult to tell what they are going through even when things are hard for them because they always seem fine, not in a withdrawn or uncaring way, but in a dynamic and involved way. You seem to feel better in their presence because they are modeling an attitude that is both inspiring and deeply fulfilling. Even if we cannot duplicate the attitude they seem to be able to carry, we can certainly move in that direction. Aligning our thoughts and desires with the goals we truly want will give us that magnetism.

The greatest demagnetizer of all is when we think, "I wish things were different so I could finally be happy! How can this be happening to me?" If you again think of those you know, you will find that the least magnetic, and least happy, people among them are those who predominantly hold defeatist and victim-oriented thoughts. And the most magnetic are those who are always looking for how to respond to a situation and never waste energy wishing it were different. Simply put, having mastered themselves they can then be more focused on doing and solving than on regretting or blaming.

When some people say they will do something, it is as good as done. With others, we've come to expect that something will distract them, and the deed will be left unfinished. Our expectation reflects the individual's lack of personal magnetism, which is a function of their words not being aligned with their thoughts, and their actions being misaligned with their speech. When we have learned to focus our mind like a laser beam instead of a floodlight, there will be almost nothing beyond our grasp. Meditation as we will see in Part II, can help us line up these various elements of ourselves so that every "mental citizen" is pointed in the same direction.

XI

OUR RESPONSE IS OUR RESPONSIBILITY

Remember the story of the blind man on the bus? We made it easy for you because we told you the person who bumped you was blind. Suppose you hadn't been able to tell? Being unable to tell is actually much more common. Here's a sobering thought to consider: Every time someone hurts us it's because he is blind. We're all blind. Every one of us has hurt someone in the past. Further, every one of us has *intentionally* hurt someone in the past.

Suppose after someone was rude to you you felt hurt. Later, I told you that his entire family had died in a car accident just the day before. You'd surely feel less upset about what he had said to you. Nothing about his behavior had changed. What changed was your perception, expectation, and level of acceptance. But suppose I then told you that I had made a mistake and it wasn't his family, but someone else's. Then you'd likely be upset with him again. Why not stop obsessing about justifying what other people do? Everything will improve if we start with ourselves first.

If we are honest, we'd have to admit that we really don't know what drives people to do most of the things they do. I scarcely know why I do some of the things I do during the day. I certainly don't know why other people do what they do. And I don't care because my primary job is to control my own mind, not to wonder about theirs. After I have centered myself I feel free to explore what I imagine are their motivations, but that comes afterwards.

People do not behave at random. We are all subject to impulses conditioned by our past learning, past experiences, and present emotions based on that history. These things make us more "robotic" and reactive and less clear and rational. This entire program is an effort to help us step outside of these conditioned patterns and constraints using our discrimination, insight, and ability to self-reflect. So when someone hurts us or behaves badly, we ought to be able to sincerely understand that the other person is somewhat "out of control," "robotic," or "blind" as well. Use whatever word helps you remember to let the other person off the hook so you can focus on yourself first. Perhaps his poor behavior was in an area that is not a weakness of ours, but we are surely blind in other areas where the "offender" is not. We're all blind, just not all in the same way. That's what makes life so interesting!

We're All Crazy

Someone once said, accurately and interestingly I believe, "We are all crazy. We just hang around with other people who are crazy in the same way we are, and then we think we're normal!" Our little group looks at a different little group and thinks, "Boy, are they peculiar." Of course they are looking at yet a third group, that is in turn looking at another, and so on. Our little group of friends may be very meticulous and never late for anything. With us, everything is in its place. We look at that group over there and realize immediately how sloppy they are – disorganized, late for things, always at a loss. We think, "How can they live that way?"

Of course they look at us and wonder how any group of people can be so uptight. According to them, we miss all the spontaneity and fun that make life worth living. And they suspect that half of us will have premature heart attacks, as our group is filled with "type A" personalities.

We feel comfortable with people who think like us. That's fine, but it can also blind us. When others do things that upset us, why not assume that they have some reason, unseen and unknown to us? After we are freed by watching the movie, then and only then can we hope to understand the other person's behavior. They, of course, see our transgressions because they occur in areas that *they* are sensitive to, and we are not. If we were sensitive to the behavior that bothered them we wouldn't do them in the first place. This is why we see everyone else's flaws and not our own. Our flaws are in our areas of blindness.

People act from an internally self-consistent set of premises. No one wakes up in the morning and thinks, "I think I'll be evil today!" Yet there are evil people in the world, and many more good people who get caught in a delusion of some sort now and then. If no one thinks they themselves are evil, then what is going on?

We are simply blinded by our desires and the compulsion to see the world as we would like it to be rather than as it is. Within our own framework, our actions always make sense. "I had to do that terrible thing because it was for the greater good," or "What else could I do after he said what he said?" The kind of introspection, clarity of vision, and calm we need to both feel better and truly see what is best to do can only come when one practices stepping back. True perspective can only be gained from removing oneself to a proper distance.

Driving at Night

Let's suppose you're driving at night to a distant city. How far ahead on the road can you see? With your headlights on, you can probably see about thirty yards. Should you strain to see beyond what the headlights show? Can you see the city you're driving to? No, but those things are of no concern.

Suppose there's a pothole fifty yards ahead. In another twenty yards you will be able to see it and swerve appropriately. In fact, if you strain to see too far up the road, you will miss what's right in front of you.

What kind of driver are you as you navigate the roadways of life? Do you worry and strain to see what cannot yet be seen thus missing what is happening right in front of you? Is your mind always in the future? We often fret that the road is not going exactly along the path we had expected or imagined, so something must be "wrong." Or is your mind stuck regretting what is in the past, constantly glancing in the rearview mirror at things that have long been settled?

The vast majority of the time we would be much better off just going calmly and confidently the thirty yards we *can* see and reconsidering everything once our perspective changes because we are now in a new place. From that new location we can see things we were unable to see previously. Stop – Breathe – Reflect – and Choose and the meditation techniques that follow are both geared towards bringing our minds to the present and helping us focus on what is right in front of us.

Often we are in a complex situation and get mentally stuck. Yet most of the time, even when it's complex, there is a step or two that is clear to take. Rather than getting stuck because we cannot see the entire picture yet, just take the step or two you know is right or necessary. After that, you will be in a slightly new "location" and may see things from your new vantage point that you hadn't previously noticed. If nothing else, you will at least have done something useful (step one) which often is just what is needed to get passed the stuck feeling.

This is, of course, not an exhortation against planning! Planning is often crucial to the success of an endeavor. But much of what we do in the name of planning is just worrying about things we have no control over and are not yet even appropriate to consider. If you have pondered the same potential roadblock three times already, you are just worrying in the name of "planning." If you have a five-step process and the only next step possible right now is step two, why focus on the others? Put your whole heart and mind into step two, and once that is done you may even view the other steps differently or see that you were originally mistaken and that the step is not even necessary. *Get* the tennis ball; don't brood over where it is, where you'd have preferred it to be, where it might be later, or where it was a few minutes ago.

Moving Energy Has Its Own Intelligence

This is a very interesting and slightly challenging phrase. It took me some years to begin to really understand. If you try it on for size, its deeper meaning may come to you also.

Too often we sit on the edge of a pool wondering whether the water is cold. In such a simple example, the solution of putting a toe in the water is somewhat obvious. Yet in our lives we often feel stuck and unable to make a move that might help clarify the decision we need to make. The idea that "moving energy has its own intelligence" has often helped me get going. Many times doing something, anything short of something totally absurd, will serve to get things going. It's like priming a pump, that first rush of which gets the pump going. Too often we fear being "wrong" so much we are frozen and unable to take even a small safe step forward because our mind immediately jumps out into the more distant future, stuck on "But what about . . .?" Take one step and get the energy moving!

A woman came to a counselor and shared what was quite a difficult situation. Her husband had left her, she had not been in the workforce in some years, and her financial situation was not good. On top of that she was having some significant, though not life-threatening, health challenges. She had always been an avid bike rider. She had the proper clothes, gear, and quite a fine bike, but had fallen away from it as her life situation did not really allow the time. She also had become fairly depressed at the turn her life had taken, and riding now seemed like more of a chore than a pleasure.

During her talk with the counselor she got some very strange-sounding advice. At one point the counselor looked at her quite intensely and said, "Honey, get on your bike!" Having spent a half hour describing the various difficulties she was facing, she naturally asked what that had to do with anything. The response came back again, "Just get on that bike – every day." The woman said she would.

Sure enough, when they saw each other a month later, things had gotten much better. It turns out that riding that bike every day got her energy moving. She felt better. The exercise helped her get out of her mood. She was doing something she was good at, which was a confidence builder. Soon, with her mood lifted, she started to see solutions where before she could only see problems. Moving energy has its own intelligence. Do anything short of lunacy, but do something!

View life as an experiment. I have always been amused that in grade "B" science fiction movies there is often a scene where the scientist is standing dejectedly in his lab. "The experiment was a failure!" he says to his assistant as if the world has ended. In a purely scientific sense, however, no experiment can be a failure. An experiment is intended to establish the truth or falsity of a hypothesis. If the experiment is set up properly, you have learned something, whether it was what you expected or wanted, or not.

Thomas Edison tried over sixteen hundred elements before finding the right substance for use as the filament in the lightbulb. His friends all told him to give up. But he figured that each one that didn't work was bringing him closer to finding the one that would work. Eventually he succeeded by keeping his energy moving forward at all times. He did not become stuck by focusing on what hadn't worked in the past; nor did he listen to his "friends" who tried to convince him to give up; nor did he become negative by blaming others or the laws of physics; he just kept driving thirty yards at a time and eventually he reached his destination.

Work vs. Service

Work and service are two closely related ideas, except that one leaves us feeling burdened, and the other leaves us feeling virtuous. "Work" is usually found in phrases like "hard work," "I have to go work," and "work for a living." "Service" is often found in phrases like, "selfless service," "performed a great service," and "a life of service." Clearly one idea leaves us feeling much better than the other!

In reality, the only difference between the two revolves around where your attention is while you are acting. We feel like we are "working" when we're thinking about ourselves. We feel like we're performing a "service" when we are thinking of the people our actions benefit. As we have previously discussed, thinking of others brings us much greater happiness and much less stress. We always feel good when we perform even a small good deed, such as helping an older person who is struggling with a heavy package. This is because while we are helping, we are not thinking of ourselves. If we were to lift the identical package, expending the same amount of energy, but thought about how we'd rather be doing something else, or that we *had* to do it, it would suddenly become "work."

Doing something for an external reward changes the action into one that is unpleasant. An interesting experiment bears directly on this point:

> A group of children were selected who especially enjoyed playing with colored felt-tipped pens. They were divided into three groups. One group was given no instructions. A second group was given a small reward if they played with the pens. The third group was promised and given substantial rewards for playing with them. When reevaluated later, the group that had been most rewarded showed the least interest in playing with the pens, while the children who had been left uninstructed showed by far the greatest interest in doing so. Further, they played happily long after the other two groups had finished.*
>
> Psychologist Edward Deci separated a group of college students into two groups. Each was asked to solve a series of puzzles, which could be assembled into hundreds of patterns. The first group was paid a dollar for each puzzle solved, while the other group received no reward. The unrewarded group continued to work with the puzzles even after the experiment officially ended, just for the joy of it. The students who received payment, meanwhile, stopped working at the earliest possible moment, and just sat or thumbed through magazines.†

---

*M. Lepper, Greene, D., & Nisbett, R. (1973), "Undermining Children's Intrinsic Interest With Extrinsic Reward: A Test of the 'Overjustification' Hypothesis," *Journal of Personality and Social Psychology* (28), 129–137.

†E. L. Deci, and R. M. Ryan, (1985), *Intrinsic Motivation and Self-Determination in Human Behavior* (New York: Plenum Press, 1985).

We must be careful that our work, which is at its root a service to someone, and our joys, which are a service to ourselves, not be transformed into solely a mercenary endeavor.

Free to Respond as We Choose

How many times have we heard someone say something like, "Well of course I gave him a piece of my mind. (not that we really have much to spare!) After what he did, how can you blame me?" The question is not, of course, how someone can blame you, but what you can do to create the most happiness in your own life. To imply you had no choice is to assert that you were acting as a robot programmed by your emotions and had lost the capacity for self-determination.

In his famous experiment, Pavlov would ring a bell for a moment before feeding a dog. This went on for some time. After a while, the dog would begin to salivate every time the bell rang in anticipation of the food. Eventually the food was no longer brought when the bell was rung, but the dog, now conditioned to this outside stimulus, would always salivate whenever it was rung anyway. If we allow ourselves, we can come to a point where we always become upset when someone does such and such or always feel stress when such and such happens. Using our minds, will, and discrimination, we can be freer than that dog. The more we can free ourselves from our conditioning and respond appropriately and freshly to every circumstance, the more we are truly free. This kind of freedom is simply incompatible with stress.

If I were sitting in a chair somewhere, and someone came up to me and said, "Get out of that chair! I want to sit there" I might be justified in saying, "What are you talking about? I was here first, and I see no reason why I should get up for you." But justified is not the point. Dale Carnegie, the great American writer and educator and an authority on how to conduct oneself, often said that one never "wins" an argument. All one does by winning is to prove a point but make an enemy. Showing you are "right" is not necessarily helpful.

I might instead choose another option. I could stand up and say something like, "Oh, I'm so sorry. I didn't know you wanted it. I'm glad to let you sit here." You'll be amazed at how often responding very graciously to an inappropriate or overbearing request changes the tenor of the situation dramatically. It's like the ancient martial art of Jujitsu, where one uses the onrush of the attacker's own energy against him, flinging him forward across the room by stepping aside at the right time and grabbing and pulling him in the direction he was going already.

If we respond in a confrontational way, we are subtly justifying the rude man's behavior. But if we respond graciously, the only element in the room that is noteworthy is the man and his bad attitude, and he may well notice this himself. Oftentimes responding to tense situations with total grace and calm is like holding up a mirror. It often jolts the other person into seeing the inappropriateness of their bad behavior.

But don't employ this as a mere trick. To do so means you are really only thinking of yourself again! The highest service you can perform for yourself is to be able to let go of the attitudes and ideas that are hurting you. It is not about the chair.

Do not memorize this strategy as your new "best" response. The point here is that if we are *truly* free, *all* responses become options, and the mere act of choosing one leaves us feeling in command and not out of control. If you always felt that you had to "stand up for yourself," you would not be free; not because you stood up for yourself, but because you *had* to. Could you have chosen to do something else or were you a robot, like a programmed piece of equipment? Once you are free, you can choose to push back or give in. But until you are free, you will feel stress and out of control even when you "win." It cannot be wrong to have freely chosen options.

How to Trigger the S – B – R – C Response

It's best to catch an emotional reaction right at the start. Once the reactive process is under way, it's much harder to step out of the pattern. This is why we often call it breaking the *cycle* of stress, since reactivity begets more reactivity. Once caught in the cycle, we become less able to choose how to respond as the whirlpool creates a drag on us.

If we can catch that moment when we start to react, we have a much better chance of being able to step back from the event. A physical cue is often a good place to start.

I have been involved with a number of organizations over the years. As is common for such groups, we have meetings to plan an event or chart a course in some area. Such meetings are an excellent time to practice Stop – Breathe – Reflect – Choose. I have learned to notice a physical cue to alert me to start the process as early as possible.

No matter how wonderful the meeting group is, I can be sure that at some point someone will suggest an idea I disagree with. There is that moment, as I have said, when I feel a perceptible tension in my chest and an urge to say something, to quash the idea lest others begin to be persuaded by it and to be sure to prevent it from taking root. That tension in the chest and urge to speak – almost like a pressure that needs to be released – is my cue. Whenever I feel that urge, I have learned to be silent instead. I will actually press my lips together whenever I first feel that chest tension. There's no way to speak then! The urge and impulse is a clear indication that I am in reactive mode and out of control. The rule of thumb might be expressed like this: *Never speak in order to relieve your own tension!* As soon as you feel that tension in your chest, it is your body's way of sending you an alert. Immediately start Stop – Breathe – Reflect – Choose because at that very moment you are on drugs! One of the two-minute breathing exercises we describe in the meditation section will help tremendously.

When we speak to release our own tension, we are surely not thinking about what is best to say. Nor are we thinking about what effect our words will have on others. We are also not asking, "What's trying to happen here." We don't even care. We just want to get rid of the tension we feel. This is an almost universal experience and has given rise to the phrase, "Let me get this off my chest." Let's face it though: the chance of our emotional reaction being the very best thing to do in that situation is remarkably small. This is the ideal time to step back, look at the movie, and decide what the actor in the movie ought to do.

There are several alternate ideas to consider apart from what you want to say:

a) Is there really a rush to speak?

b) Could the other person's idea actually be right?

c) Might someone else oppose the idea thus getting you off the hook?

d) Might it die of its own weight without anyone saying anything?

e) Even if a bad idea, might it spur someone else to have a winning idea?

There are many possibilities that you will have short-circuited if you instantly react and jump on what was just said. Further, reacting emotionally will endear you to no one. People do not like to have their ideas or thoughts immediately contradicted. Dale Carnegie referred to confrontation as being "angular." It never pays directly to contradict someone else. There is always a way to steer the conversation in a better direction, rather than just directly negating the previous thought. It seems clear that this sort of finesse and tact is only possible when we are in control of our reactive process and able to step back and see clearly what the other person can actually hear right now, what the other person may have truly meant, what he holds dear, what he will resist giving up, etc.

A friend of mine was responsible for planning the development of a small town in rural Northern California. He had to decide where to put a path that needed to cut across a large open field. Everyone seemed to have a different opinion as to where it should go and how it should be shaped. But he had another way to approach the question. He waited until the field was cleared and did nothing. Since the field was between two points of destination, people just started walking across the grass rather than walking around the field. He then observed where the paths naturally were created and put the permanent paths close to where people had walked. He was able to move people a bit, but had he put the paths where he liked and nowhere near where people wanted to walk, most people would have just cut across the field and forged their own paths. His approach went along with human nature, nudging it slightly, rather than trying to change it wholesale.

Humility

The approach to life we have been discussing will also engender within us one of the sweetest and magnetic personal qualities someone can develop: humility. By humility I do not mean the kind of self-deprecating pose that some people put on. Nor do I mean the kind where the person in question seems to feel that his deep sense of humility is his crowning achievement, always aware of how well his humility suits him and plays to others. I mean the genuine kind that we always find inspiring because the person wears it like a comfortable sweater. It comes as part of a true understanding that we are all on this planet together, doing the very best we can to find the peace and happiness that is our birthright. Everyone has different talents, abilities, intelligence, and gifts, not to speak of backgrounds, upbringings, life experiences, and histories.

Our worth as a person is not based merely on the skills we possess, nor the things we have learned. One who can clearly see this lives a life of humility doing service wherever and whenever he can, because he sees each person he meets as a brother or sister. When such a person is wronged by someone, he is more likely to think, "I'm glad I don't have that unfortunate quality of his that resulted in such poor behavior," rather than, "How could he do that to me? What's wrong with him, anyway." I think it is easy to see how one attitude leads toward peace and contentment while the other towards judgment, anger, and frustration.

In Conclusion

I hope you have found a few ideas that touched you or enabled you to see yourself and the world in a different way. It is not necessary to implement all the ideas and methods that have been described in these pages. Find a few with which you feel at home and put your energy into those. Like troops establishing a breach into enemy territory, get a toehold in some new concept and pour your troops into the opening created. Please don't focus on the things that seemed unclear or misguided to you, as such a focus will not help you. Hopefully at least a few pages inspired you to make a fresh start on how you approach your day. The next move is up to you. It has been said that a room can be in darkness for a thousand years, but the instant a light is turned on, all darkness immediately vanishes. All things will improve if you make an effort starting now. Best wishes on your new adventure.

Part II

INTRODUCTION TO PART II

M editation is a remarkable practice. All the necessary equipment is within you; your breath is all that is required. Given that it takes less time than a standard session of working out, jogging, or playing tennis, its effects on both physical and mental health are quite striking. Meditation has now been clinically proven to have beneficial results when used to combat heart disease, diabetes, insomnia, asthma, chronic pain, mood swings, high blood pressure, and a host of other ailments. And though newly accepted in the West, it has been a familiar practice throughout much of the world for many thousands of years. The simplicity, ease of practice, powerful beneficial results, and scientific support that meditation has now garnered goes a long way towards explaining its widespread popularity in the United States as well. There are ten million people in the United States who meditate regularly, and many millions more around the world.

Meditation is a simple practice of breathing in a certain way, repeated over time, that has tremendous beneficial effects for both the body and the mind. It can bring us back towards proper functioning and health. Since we get pushed out of balance every day from the stressors we each face, a brief session of rebalancing the body's systems works wonders in enabling it to effectively deal with or heal many physical ailments. The body is always fighting on our behalf, and meditation gives it an extra boost to win in its battle against infirmities. A session of meditation is like tuning a musical instrument. We can retune our bodies so that they are playing at just the right pitch.

Meditation and Stress

Stress depresses our immune system. When we are under stress, it's as if we were fighting a war on two fronts. It is similar to the feeling of sluggishness that comes after a big meal. Much of our body's energy is going into digesting the food we have just eaten. When we are under stress, the body behaves poorly as our energy goes to maintain the body's equilibrium in the face of the stress onslaught. Thus stress inhibits physical immune responses, stamina, and general health. In one study, medical students under stress during exam periods were taught meditation. The more they practiced, the higher the percentage of T-helper cells circulating in their blood (cells that arouse the immune response to fight off infection).*

---

*J. Kiecolt-Glaser, R. Glaser, E. Strain, et al., "Modulation of Cellular Immunity in Medical Students," *Journal of Behavioral Medicine* (1986), 9:311–20.

The Physiology of Meditation

Each cell of the body consumes oxygen in order to burn food. The collective amount needed by this cellular process is what we call "metabolism." A greatly decreased level of metabolism is called "hypometabolism," which is a deeply restful and rejuvenating state for the body and is only caused by two activities: sleep and meditation.

In sleep, the body's metabolism slowly decreases. After three to four hours one enters a state of hypometabolism. At this point oxygen consumption drops about eight percent from normal waking levels. The time we spend in this sleep-induced hypometabolic state is what enables sleep to refresh us physically.

During meditation the drop in oxygen consumption is almost immediate. Further, the drop is in the 10–20 percent range, as opposed to 8 percent during sleep. Meditation is the only activity scientists have found that creates such a deep hypometabolic state and thus such a deep state of restfulness.

Studies have also shown that people who practice meditation regularly generally need *less* sleep. This is particularly interesting if you think you don't have time to meditate. You may get back the time spent meditating by simply sleeping a little less!

A further interesting and beneficial consequence of meditation regards the brain function of meditators. The brain generates several types of waves that are easily measurable by an EEG (electro-encephalogram). The waves that indicate the best balance between a sense of peace and alert attention are called alpha waves. Alpha waves are also the level of brain activity most associated with positive moods. These waves are also present when we see the world objectively. That is, when we are generating alpha waves, and are thus more receptive and non-agitated, we tend to see the world for what it is rather than through the distorting filter of our emotions.

Alpha waves are present when we are meditating, and meditation is the best way to generate them. Sleep is restful physically (hypometabolism always is) but doesn't generally leave us with the truly *positive* feeling and outlook that a conscious alpha-wave generating activity (meditation) does. Sleep simply gives us some relief from the problems of the day for a little while.

A Harvard Medical School study found that meditation decreases oxygen consumption, heart rate, respiratory rate, and blood pressure, and increases the intensity of alpha, theta, and delta brain waves – the opposite of the physiological changes that occur during the stress response.*

Recent advances in our ability to map the brain show that meditation also changes how the brain functions. Different areas of the brain are active in different circumstances. Brain activity is indicated by increased neural firings in different locations, which can now be seen by using an fMRI (functional magnetic resonance imager). When we are feeling good, the left half of the prefrontal lobe is active. One can think of that part of the prefrontal lobe as a switch that keeps negative emotions in check and inhibits their ability to take over.

The second part of the brain to consider here is the limbic system, which is active when strong emotions are present (aggression, fear, anger, etc.).

---

*Herbert Benson, "The Relaxation Response," Harvard Medical School (New York: HarperTorch 1976).

By their nature, then, these two parts of the brain are in opposition. That is, when one is active, the other is quiet and vice versa. Almost all people who are under extreme stress have heightened activity in the limbic system and reduced activity in the "feel good" prefrontal lobe. "Almost all people" because meditators have a different brain pattern. When people who have practiced meditation over a long period of time are studied, one finds that their prefrontal lobes are active and their limbic systems are quiet, even in extreme situations. The more regular the practice and the more experienced the practitioner, the more profound the effect. Simply put, meditators have retrained their brains to keep negative emotions and reactions from dominating their brain functions, rather than allowing them to take over. It is no wonder then that meditators seem calmer than most people. The practice has rewired their brains to be that way.

Heightened Awareness and Involvement

Quieting our emotional reactivity would not be useful if it came by decreasing our awareness of circumstances. Some people may be calm because they don't know what's going on! Yet at the same time that meditation quiets our emotional reactivity, it also enhances our alertness and ability to engage with the world around us. An experiment was performed where a group of meditators were shown an extremely violent movie. The same movie was shown to a group of people who had never practiced meditation. One result we might have expected: the meditators had less of a physiological reaction to the movie. That is, they showed less stress as evidenced by a smaller heart rate increase, less perspiration, less muscle tension, and a smaller increase of oxygen consumption. But the more interesting result was that the meditators could tell the researchers *more* about the movie when it was over. They were less stressed *and* more aware of the movie's details than the non-meditators. Rather than dulling their awareness in some sort of a dreamy state, meditation made them able to be more receptive and observant of the world around them and more engaged with what was happening in front of them. Meditation practices can lead to heightened cortical arousability plus decreased limbic arousability, so that perception is heightened and emotion is simultaneously reduced.*

Researchers also tested novice meditators on a button-pressing task requiring speed and concentration. Performance was greater at 40 minutes of meditation than after a 40-minute nap.†

Martial Arts For the Mind

A martial artist is intensely aware of his surroundings as is the meditator. As we have seen, skilled meditators are calmer, less reactive, and more observant than the average person. The practice of meditation cuts down on the "static" that most people have in their minds. While

---

*Michael Murphy and Steven Donovan, The Physical and Psychological Effects of Meditation (Institute of Noetic Sciences, 1997).
†(Reported by Carey Goldberg, *The Boston Globe*, Nov. 23, 2005.

trying to concentrate on a task or an element of their surroundings, most people have hundreds of background-interrupting thoughts such as, "I wonder what time it is? I wonder what I should make for dinner? I wonder if so-and-so is back yet?" Wouldn't it be great to have your mind under your command; the ability to focus it whenever and wherever you choose? Meditation enables you to improve your ability to focus the mind to a fine point of concentration. When a martial artist approaches a stack of bricks to perform one of the remarkable feats for which he is known, such as shattering ten bricks stacked vertically with a single blow of the hand, the first thing he does is get his mind fully engaged in the process by focusing and shutting out all other thoughts.

This kind of single-mindedness comes from years of mental discipline as much as the physical practice required for such feats. The body without the mind can do nothing. If you watch such a martial arts demonstration, you will see that for some time before every feat, the martial artist will stand motionless before the task at hand breathing, perhaps even with eyes closed, marshalling all his thoughts and will into a single point, and then striking rapidly with force. Without that mental discipline and focus he would be unable to accomplish his task and might well hurt himself in the process.

Energy is Outward All Day

We send enormous energy out of our body through our senses every day. We hear external sounds, we see external sights, and we feel external objects. This has a draining effect over time. Meditation is an opportunity to reverse that constant outward flow of consciousness. It is why meditation is done in a quiet space, without "background" music, motionless, and with our eyes closed. These factors give us the opportunity to lessen the never-ending input from external stimulation.

A number of medical traditions recommend a brief fast occasionally. One of the benefits of this practice is that such a routine rests the digestive system, which otherwise is constantly working. The heart has a natural small rest between contracting and expanding in the process of pumping blood. Why not also give our mind a rejuvenating kind of rest from its constant task of processing external stimuli? Sleep is one form of rest, but meditation is one that can be done during the day as needed and has many ancillary benefits that sleep will never provide.

Meditation as Mental Exercise

We do a lot for our bodies: we try to eat well, get the rest we need, exercise, and see a doctor if we are not well. But what do we do for our minds? By this I do not mean the intellectual mind through crossword puzzles, challenges at work, and the like. What we are speaking about here is overall mental fitness.

Many people work out every day. Yet the mind is at least as important as the body; it needs care just as our physical selves do in order to function smoothly. How many people work to strengthen and tone this most important part of the body? Meditation is the best exercise anyone has ever developed for the mind.

Like the body, the mind can bump along without any special attention and not seem to cause problems, but we know that a body that works out is stronger, healthier, and more attractive. The physical body is easy to see, and pain is easy to experience, so the physical body gets all of our attention. Our mental condition is more abstract and much harder to measure, so the mind tends to be ignored until a crisis hits.

Our Bodies Respond to Our Will

What would it be like if you were speaking with someone and your feet suddenly decided to leave the room? Of course, this can't happen because our bodies respond to our will. But what about your mind? When you have a difficult interaction with someone, what do you spend the next few hours (or days or months) thinking about? Wouldn't it be nice if you could say to your mind, "Enough! Thinking about this is useless, and I need to focus on what I'm doing!" But we often can't get our minds to go where we want. We *can* have much more control over our minds, however, if we learn how and practice.

Newborns are not familiar with how the body works. We buy them colored toys of many shapes and sizes to play with and manipulate so that over time, as they explore the world around them, they learn not only how other things work but also how to control their own bodies. Every day is filled with excited exploration of how the body and this world it inhabits work.

A similar situation is true for our minds. But whereas it quickly becomes clear if the body is not under our control, it is more difficult to recognize the same condition for our minds. We can often get by with a lower level of mental control, focus, and clarity. Since the frustration is usually less, we put our attention and energy elsewhere. Since the results of not having a workout routine for the mind is generally neither devastating nor obvious, we can go for an entire lifetime without addressing our overall mental state. Of course, if the stress gets so great we feel we *have* to face it, we sometimes do.

When things go wrong in our lives, it is more difficult for us to trace the cause to our mental attitudes and general state of mind. The cause-and-effect relationship is simply not as clear as it is with the body, though surely no less real. This means that whereas the infant has tremendous incentive to get the body working and to behave as he wants, it *appears* we have much less incentive to have the mind fall under our control in the same way.

Meditation is to the mind as working out is to the body. Fortunately, many of the fruits of meditation come more quickly. If you start a diet, for example, and after one day of following its recommendations, you run to check your weight on a scale, you are likely to be disappointed! But a large number of our students have noted significant changes after even one session of meditation. This is wonderful because it gives us an immediate incentive to continue our practice, whereas a diet takes a certain amount of faith. I know a number of people who say that if they miss their session of meditation in the morning, they just don't feel quite as good for the rest of the day.

Remember the woman who had chronic migraines since she was eight years old? After taking our program, she reported that for the first time in her life she had been able to eliminate her migraines without taking drugs. Another woman wrote to us the day after attending to say that she slept through the entire night for the first time in years. These people had all the incentive they needed to continue their practice. Unfortunately, when a difficulty is not as specific as pain or insomnia, it is harder to trace it back to our stress level and thus the incentive is not as clear.

Meditation and Creativity

Have you ever awakened at two in the morning with the solution to a problem that has been troubling you for a long time? Or had an insight while you were doing something relaxing that was totally unrelated to the situation involving the insight? Or perhaps you remembered something suddenly while long past the time you wanted that bit of information? What happens in those occurrences is that the mind has relaxed and opened, either during sleep or while relaxed in another setting. The mental chatter had been stilled. The part of the mind that worries, "Yes, but . . ." when new thoughts and ideas arise, had been quieted.

It is similar to what happens during brainstorming. Participants are asked to present ideas without criticism from others. The ideas can be analyzed later. Everyone understands that most of the ideas will not be used, and that many will not even be practical. But like priming a pump, just being able to voice ideas results in a greater flow. Typically, a few turn out to be quite good.

If each idea were discussed, debated, and dissected, and possibly rejected as soon as it came up, little creativity would flourish. The kind of thinking that encourages idea formation is not the kind that finds flaws in each idea as soon as it is presented. The two approaches are simply not compatible.

Stress is a major block to one's natural creativity. Mental chatter and distractions block the natural flow of openness to ideas and inspiration just as debating each idea kills successful brainstorming. Creativity-destroying chatter and mental distractions are found in abundance in the untrained mind. One cannot be intuitive when filled with worry, doubt, fear, or stress. Meditation gives us the tools we need to get the mind to behave and be still, thus enabling the creative process to continue naturally and unhindered.

The analytical mind needs to be used in conjunction with creativity and intuition to check what has been developed, but ought not to be used either too early or in too heavy-handed a way. Without the mental discipline and control meditation develops for us, letting creativity develop is difficult since the analytical mind is always looking for something to do and cannot resist jumping in and shouting its opinions.

The analytical mind analyzes and pulls apart. It sees problems and impracticalities. The calmly creative and intuitive mind sees solutions and possibilities. They need to work together, but one without the other will always yield inferior results.

Meditation opens up a new world to us and develops our mind in ways that other practices cannot. One can use these newfound insights and perceptions in many ways: in the arts, in business, in sports, and in one's own spiritual practices.

Meditation and Spirituality

Meditation is a part of many spiritual traditions. Even religions not normally associated with meditation, like Christianity, have meditative branches, or have had sects in the past that had meditation as a key practice. The question naturally arises then, why is this? In the same way that intuition can only occur with a calm heart, so too, can God's presence only be felt with a calm heart. Many believe that when Jesus said, "Be still and know," it is meditation to which he is referring, because true perception can only come when the mind is still. "The kingdom of God is within you" also seems to suggest an inner place of awareness that meditation can access and which many believe to be a doorway to the Infinite.

Different Types of Meditation

There are many different types of meditation though they all have the breath and mental focus in common. When clinically tested, however, the benefits appear to be essentially the same. So find a type that appeals to you and then practice it regularly. It is far better to be regular in your practice than to experiment endlessly with the minor differences. It is more important to commit to your practice and get going in earnest.

XII

MEDITATION PRACTICES

Step 1: Light Stretching

Before you sit to meditate, you will want to stretch and relax. You can do any kind of stretching that you like. Your body will tell you what you need. If you know yoga, you can do a few poses. Yoga was originally developed as a way to relax the body in preparation for meditation and is ideal for this purpose. If you have our guided meditation CD, you'll be guided to do the following, with your eyes closed:

- Stretch the arms overhead and arch the back, taking a deep inhalation. Then exhale and relax the arms back down to your sides.
- Place your hands on your shoulders and do a few shoulder rotations in one direction. Then reverse. Make large slow circles and "wring" any tension out of the shoulder area.
- Do gentle neck rolls, turning the head five times in a small, relaxed circle. Then reverse. If your neck is at all sensitive to injury, raise your shoulders as you do

this and make the circles small. If you hear a small clicking sound, don't worry. This is natural and will become quieter or disappear as you gain greater flexibility and relaxation in the neck.

Benefits: Your body will be happier to sit and cooperate with you rather than complaining about little aches and pains along the way.

Step 2: Tensing and Relaxing the Muscles

Stand with the legs about shoulder-width apart. Close the eyes, take a deep inhalation, then hold the breath and tense all the muscles in the body. Then exhale, and relax. Do this three times, and then begin to work with individual muscle groups.

- Start with the left foot; tense gradually to a peak of tension, and then relax gradually
- Go to the right foot, do the same
- Left calf, then right
- Left thigh, then right
- Left hip and buttock, then right
- Lower abdomen
- Stomach
- Make a fist with the left hand, and tense the left forearm. Then do the same with the right
- Left upper arm, then right
- Left side of chest, then right
- Shoulders (lift them toward the ears and tense, then gently drop and relax)
- Neck
- All the muscles of the face.

• Take a deep inhalation, exhale, shaking loose the arms and legs

Benefits: This exercise helps to reduce blood pressure and to increase circulation. It can be done standing, or in any position, even lying down. Practice tensing and relaxing while seated on airplanes to alleviate cramping and fatigue. You can use it in the morning while still in bed to help slowly awaken the body and prepare it to joyfully (or at least willingly) hop out of bed.

Step 3: Setting the Pose

Go ahead and sit down now. All that's necessary is that the spine be upright and straight. You can sit in a

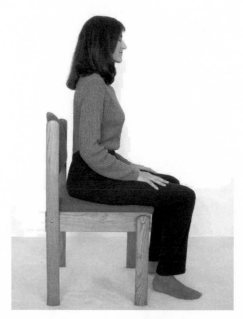

Figure 1. Correct sitting position.

dining room chair with a padded seat, or any straight-backed chair you wish, preferably without arms. Sit perched at the front edge of the chair.

This is so you don't feel anything touching your body but the seat of the chair. It is not unusual for your back to become tired in this position. If this happens, you may wish to place a small pillow under the buttocks to lift them, so they are higher than the thighs. This releases tension in the lower back.

If you find your back still becomes tired, slide back with your back all the way against the back of the chair for support, but keep the spine straight as you do this. (For a fuller discussion about how to establish the most comfortable sitting position for you, see pages 164–170).

Figure 2. Back against chair with spine straight.

Draw the shoulders back, expand the chest area, and allow the stomach to become soft and relaxed. Set the chin parallel to the floor. Close your eyes and turn your gaze slightly upward, as if you were looking at a point just a bit above the horizon line. Keep your eyes in this slightly upraised position, and then do not think about them. Be sure it is only the eyes that are slightly upturned and not the head. If your neck gets stiff or tense over time, you have probably tilted your head.

Mentally, step back from the body and become an observer. Observe without judgment how the body responds to each technique, as if you were a scientist conducting an experiment on yourself.

Visualize a strong cord running through the center of the body, along the spine, and passing out through the top of the head. Allow all the bones and muscles to hang comfortably on that strong central support.

Benefits: Better posture and relaxation of the diaphragm to allow for deep breathing. Avoids slumping, which results in sleepiness.

Step 4: Full Body Scan (deep physical relaxation, consciously directed by the mind)

Inhale, hold the breath for as long as you wish, tensing all the muscles in the body. Then exhale and relax. Do this twice more. Then begin breathing naturally, through the nostrils if possible. If your nasal passages are blocked, then breathe through the mouth instead.

Bring your awareness to the left foot, name that body part mentally, and ask the muscles there to relax. Don't tense the muscle physically as we did before. Just say to yourself, "Foot, relax." Then go to the right foot and do the same. Work your way up the body in the same order we did in Step 2. Simply issue the mental command and observe the result. If there is no change, fine. If there is a slight release or shift in tension, enjoy that release. You will find that even a small shift brings significant release of physical tension and often of chronic pain. After you get up to the neck, add these additional steps:

- Allow the jaw to drop open and relax
- Mouth and tongue, relax
- Cheeks, relax
- Temples and forehead, relax
- Eyes and eyelids, relax
- Scalp, relax
- Finally, relax the brain. Promise the mind that you'll come back to projects and plans soon. But for now, allow the mind to be here, now, observing and aware.

When finished with the full body scan, do a quick overall scan of the body and notice if any parts have become tense once again. Name that body part and ask the muscles there to relax.

Benefits: Relief of tension and chronic pain. As you do this exercise, you will begin to notice parts of the body that chronically carry tension. They are your forward guards and are the first to bear the brunt of it when you feel stress. Thank them for keeping you notified, and then allow them to relax from their duties. They will be able to relax and release you from the tension and even severe pain once they know they have your attention.

Note: You can use this exercise while in bed at night to overcome insomnia. Just turn your eyes downward rather than upward. If upon completing the body scan you are still awake, do it again slowly. If still awake, practice "Watching the Breath" as described below until asleep.

Step 5: Equal Measured Breathing

Inhale slowly for a count of five, hold the breath for five, and then exhale slowly for five. Begin again right away without pause, inhaling, holding, and exhaling. Do this all through the nostrils if possible. It is best to contract the throat slightly as if you were humming a note, but without the audible sound. Practice this on your own a little before starting the technique. Hum a note out loud. Then holding all the same muscles in the same way, exhale without the audible tone. You may hear the air coming in and out through the slightly contracted throat.

What brings the benefit is the equality of the breath. The volume of air is unimportant. This is not a deep breathing exercise. The reason for the slight contraction of the throat is that it enables us to make the inhalations and exhalations longer than normal. It is the length of these that determines the level of relaxation. That is, an inhalation of five counts, hold five counts, and an exhalation of five counts, brings more benefit than doing each part for three counts. But this is not a competitive sport! It's important to stay relaxed. Trying to do eighteen, eighteen, and eighteen won't win anything and may leave you feeling a little dizzy. If you ever do feel dizzy, you can stop the practice, take in a smaller volume of air, or change the count.

Remind the stomach to be relaxed. On the inhalation, allow the stomach to relax outward, away from the spine. On the exhalation, gently draw the stomach in toward the spine.

Benefits: Helps to calm strong emotional states, including fear and anger. Use it right before a stressful event, or as soon as you

notice that you are in the middle of a strong emotional response.
A few rounds of this breathing can help calm the nervous system
quickly. If you feel butterflies before speaking or singing in public,
practice a few rounds of this technique just as you are walking
onto the stage, and it will calm the adrenaline rush, giving you
more control and improved stage presence.

Step 6: Watching the Breath

Take a deep inhalation and then exhale fully. Breathe naturally without counting. When the breath begins to flow again of its own accord, begin to observe its movement, without any attempt to control it. Notice the point where the breath enters the body wherever that may be— whether at the tip of the nose, higher up in the nasal passage, the forehead, or any point you feel it coming into the body. Be an impartial observer, not caring whether it flows in or out or remains stationary. Simply remain attentive to whatever the breath does by itself, naturally.

On the inhalation, mentally say the words, "I am." On the exhalation, mentally say, "peace." You may use any phrase you wish in place of these. Examples would be "A-men" or "Still-ness." The repetition of a word or phrase gives the mind something to focus on, which is helpful for pushing aside distracting thoughts. If the breath becomes still at any point, enjoy that as a period of rest, or peace.

When you notice the mind wandering, gently bring it back to watching the movement of breath on the body. (For ideas about how to work with thoughts during meditation, see page 175.)

Benefits: This exercise helps to slow the heart rate, which in turn, slows the breath. When the breath becomes slower, you'll find that the mind's chatter slows as well. This exercise also helps increase your focus and concentration. Eventually, you'll be able to direct your mind where you want it to go because of the practice you've given your mind during meditation.

Step 7: After the Techniques

After practicing watching the breath, take a deep inhalation and exhale fully. Then sit without practicing any technique for as long as you wish. Some people use this as a period of quiet, prayer, visualization, or for the practice of an affirmation.

Benefits: You may find that your intuition is strengthened; as the mind becomes quiet, the intuition can be heard more easily. Some people keep a small pad of paper by their side during meditation to capture creative ideas or solutions to problems that may suddenly occur during these times.

Tips for Sitting Comfortably:

There are many ways to sit. Experiment to see which is best for you. The key is to have the spine straight. Most of us are not used to standing or sitting with good posture. Don't be discouraged if the body is not used to these positions yet. With just a little practice, sitting upright will become easier. Learning how to sit for meditation will benefit you greatly in learning to sit and walk with good posture at other times of the day. This, in turn, helps the body's health in many ways: removing unnecessary pressure from internal organs, increasing circulation, and increasing oxygen to the body through deeper breathing.

The secret to sitting upright without strain is finding the point of balance where your spine remains upright almost without effort. When you were a child, you may have enjoyed the game of taking a long stick or broom and holding one end in your palm, trying to keep the stick balanced straight up in the air without falling. If you were successful, you found the spot where it would stay balanced for a few seconds. That's the balance point we're looking for with our spine, and which promises an upright, comfortable position for far longer.

You can achieve this sitting in a chair, sitting on the floor, or sitting on a cushion or meditation bench designed for this purpose. As we have said, in any of these sitting positions, most people are more comfortable if they place a pillow under the buttocks to lift them higher than the thighs. The height of the pillow is individual, and you should experiment until you find the right level for you.

People often ask if they can meditate while lying down. While it is true that your spine will be straight in this position, it's not recommended for meditation, unless you are ill and are not able to sit up. The reason is twofold. First, the habit of sleep is a deep one. Most people find themselves asleep before they even realize it, once they lie down and relax. And second, meditation is an active state of intense awareness. It is easiest to achieve this in an upright position.

To establish the most comfortable position is very individual. Here are the possibilities for you to explore:

Sitting in a Chair

Most people find it easiest and most comfortable to sit in a chair to meditate. Earlier, we described a chair without arms and with a flat, padded seat like a dining room chair. Your feet should reach the floor. If the legs dangle in the air, find some books for the feet to rest on as they should always be flat on the ground during meditation. If you can, it is preferred to sit at the front edge of the chair using your spine for support, rather than the chair back, but this may be difficult for many people. If you can't support your spine sitting on the edge of the chair, then sit all the way back against the back of the chair. In either case you may find it helpful to use a pillow that's higher at the back of the chair, sloping slightly downward toward the front. This raises the buttocks slightly without raising the thighs. This posture often relieves tension in the lower back and makes sitting for meditation more comfortable.

To set the spine so it is strong and supporting the whole body without strain, sit upright, chest expanded and shoulders drawn back a bit. Tilt your pelvis forward and backward until you find a good spot that allows the spine to easily support the body. You will know when you have found the balance point because you will be able to relax the abdomen and the shoulders easily, and your posture will remain unchanged.

You have probably seen a chair specially designed to help people with lower back conditions. It's often called a "kneeler" or "back chair" and has a sloped seat for the buttocks and a padded sloped area below for the knees. These are comfortable for meditating and are usually adjustable.

Note: Sitting in a reclining chair is tempting, but will likely put you to sleep in a hurry as it is hard to keep the spine straight. We don't recommend it for this reason.

Sitting On the Floor

This is the classic image of meditation. Some extremely flexible young person is sitting cross-legged, spine erect, on some beautiful tropical beach. But this is not a comfortable sitting position for most people. To sit for any length of time in comfort, you will want a firm pillow. It can be as high or as low as you wish, and you'll need to experiment until you find the right height. You can fold a bed pillow once or twice to get the desired height and firmness. Or you can buy something designed for meditating. We use a crescent-shaped pillow with a kapok filling that is about 6" in the back and slopes down to about 3" in the front. This can be purchased at any store that carries yoga props or large metaphysical books and gift stores.

Figure 3. Meditation cushion.

Now arrange your legs to sit cross-legged. Don't sit with one ankle on top of another, as you'll soon feel one foot falling asleep. Rather, sit with one ankle in front of the other at floor level. Here's how: Hold one leg by the ankle and draw it all the way in so it's tucked right up against the groin (or as close as you can get without any strain). Then do the same with the other ankle. Bring it in and place it in front of the other ankle. Then allow the legs to relax and the knees to go down toward the ground. The higher the pillow, the easier it will be for your knees to get all the way down to the ground, making a good, stable platform for meditation.

Find the right height of pillow and spine position by sitting upright, chest expanded, and shoulders drawn back a bit. Tilt your pelvis forward and backward until you find a good spot that allows the spine to easily support the body.

Figure 4. On floor with cushion.

Figure 5. On floor – side view.

Figure 6. Legs under buttocks with cushion.

Figure 7. Cross-legged with cushion.

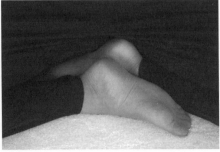

If sitting cross-legged on the floor is not comfortable for you, you are among the vast majority of people in western countries. Don't worry about it in the least, and go back to sitting in a chair. Or you may wish to try this last option:

Sitting on a Meditation Bench

Kneel on the floor, place a small bench under the buttocks, and sit. The bench should have a slanted top so that the buttocks are higher than the thighs. Many men seem to find this more comfortable than sitting on a pillow on the floor. It's also a perfect "build-it-yourself" project. Add a pad or pillow on top for extra comfort and hinges to the legs if you want to make it portable for travel. See directions above for establishing the balance point for the spine.

How to Make These Practices a Regular Part of Your Life

1) Regularity of time

Like any habit, the more you can establish a pattern, the easier it will be to do. Find a time that is best for you and meditate at that time each day whenever you can. Many people find the first thing in the morning to be the easiest for a few reasons: You tend to wake up at about the same time each day. The stomach is empty. And since you've just slept, you're (hopefully) rested and alert.

However, some people find it too chaotic at home and choose to meditate at work, before others arrive, or at noon before lunch. Some prefer to wind down after work

Figure 8. Meditation bench.

Figure 9. Starting to sit.

Figure 10. Sitting with bench.

with a meditation practice, so they can switch gears and be more fully with their families at home. Finally, some people enjoy meditating before bedtime. This is one of the most peaceful times of the day, and a way to review and release the stresses of the day completely before going to sleep.

Whatever time you choose, you'll find it's easiest to meditate on an empty stomach-before eating or two to three hours after a meal.

2) Regularity of location

Set aside a room, or small part of a room, just for meditation. You will find over time that just entering that spot begins to draw the mind towards meditation. Try to find as quiet a spot as possible-or if this is difficult, try using comfortable "foam" earplugs or headphones to block out noise. Be sure the room is not stuffy and is kept a bit on the cool side; a blanket or shawl to wrap yourself is helpful. Fresh air is ideal when possible. (Note: You can buy earplugs in any drug or hardware store. Quality headphones can be found in gun shops.)

3) Light Exercise

You should be alert and relaxed before starting your practice. Light exercise is very helpful for this, so stretch a bit before you meditate. Yoga postures were invented, thousands of years ago, specifically to relax the body in preparation for meditation. Whatever you do, it should be calming rather than vigorous. The idea is to use the exercise to both energize yourself and rid the body of some physical tension. You ought to feel more awake and alert after the exercise than before.

4) What to do with your hands

You can place your hands in any of these positions:

• Palms upturned, tucked up against the hip bone and resting on the lap. This position may feel awkward at first, but it quickly becomes natural, and makes it easier to expand the chest and to draw the shoulders slightly back. This is the preferred pose, so long as you are comfortable this way.

Figure 11. Hands with palms upturned.

• Palms face down on the thighs, but close enough to the hipbone that you can remain sitting with the spine straight. If the palms rest too far toward the knees, the shoulders will begin to come forward as well.

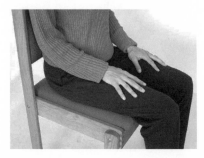

Figure 12. Hands with palms down.

• Hand in hand near the groin. This position may be most comfortable for people with long arms.

Figure 13. Hands folded in lap.

5) How Long to Meditate?

To start, meditate for at least 10 to 15 minutes each day to help develop a regular habit, and then increase your time as you wish. We have found that when a beginner has a guided meditation CD to work with, a total of a half hour for the stretching and breathing combined seems to work for almost everyone. But remember this helpful tip: Meditate as long as you are enjoying it. That way you will leave each meditation looking forward to the next session. There is no "break point." That is, there is no fixed point at which the benefits kick in. The longer the better so long as you can maintain a pleasant attitude about doing it. This will increase the likelihood that each experience is a positive one, and that when it is time to do the practice, there will be minimal mental resistance.

Toughing it out past the point of enjoyment is more likely to result in abandoning the practice. But be sensible. If you've been sitting for two minutes and feel like you're done, you may want to hang in there for another few minutes!

6) Tips for Sitting Still

Just as you are starting the sitting portion of your practice and you have gotten comfortable, mentally command the body to sit completely still for just three minutes. Speak as though you were a parent giving a firm command to a child (the body). Interestingly, the body seems to respond when it knows you mean business, and it will sit still. And once you have accomplished this, the body is very likely to continue without giving you any difficulty. Mentally check the body from time to time to relax any part that has become tense. Be relaxed, yet aware.

7) How to Work With Thoughts

The first step is to accept that the mind will wander. Don't judge yourself. Simply notice distracting thoughts whenever you are able to catch them. Gently bring your awareness back to whatever breathing technique you are practicing. Ask the mind to relax. When the mind wanders, repeat this step again. Gradually, you will become increasingly able to watch the mind without becoming entangled in its chatter. And gradually, the mind will become more and more quiet.

A helpful image: Imagine that your thoughts are like a cloud passing overhead and gently moving on out of your mental landscape. Don't focus on the cloud or resist it. Just notice it floating into the mind and passing out again.

Meditation helps you access that part of yourself that is untouched by the chaos of the world. Feel as though you are an observer of your life, your body, and your mind. Step back from the body mentally, as if you were watching it from a short distance away. You will learn to observe the movement of the mind just as you are observing the body, noticing tension, and asking the body to release it. This separation from mental chatter will give you a sense of freedom and control. You will find it easier to direct your mind where you want it to go, or to replace the sometimes destructive chatter of a fearful mind with new, more productive, and helpful ideas.

You can imagine your thoughts to be like weights in a gym. When lifting weights, you do not fret that the weights are heavy. If they weren't, they wouldn't be building your muscles! So too with your thoughts. It is their presence that gives your mind something to push against. Every time you notice you are thinking, you can bring your mind back to watching your breath. Like training a puppy to sleep in his box, every time he gets out you just patiently put him back. A moment later he is out and back he goes. Every time your mind wanders you bring it back to your breath. No judgment. It's just what minds do. Over time this exercise builds that muscle, and your mind gets the idea that it is good to respond to your will.

APPENDIX

RESEARCH ON STRESS AND MEDITATION

Stress and health

* Harvard researchers believe that 60–90 percent of doctor's visits are caused by stress.[1] Stress is linked to heart attacks, hypertension, diabetes, asthma, chronic pain, allergies, headache, backache, various skins disorders, cancer, accidents, suicide, depression, immune system weakness, decreases in the number of white blood cells and changes in their function.[2]

Heart disease

* People who suffer from chronic stress at work have an increased risk of developing heart disease and diabetes. Men who held stressful jobs for more than fourteen years were almost twice as likely to have insulin intolerance, high blood pressure, high cholesterol, and be obese than those not exposed to consistent stress.[3]
British Medical Journal

* Stress is more powerful than diet in influencing cholesterol levels. Several studies – including one of medical students around

exam time, and another of accountants during tax season – have shown significant increases in cholesterol levels during stressful events, when there was little change in diet.[4]
Homeostasis in Health and Disease

* Severe stress may be a potent risk factor for stroke even 50 years after the initial trauma. In a study of 556 veterans of WWII, the rate of stroke among those who had been prisoners of war was 8 times higher than among those not captured.[5]
Yale Medical School

* Men with above-average blood pressure spikes in response to a stressful life event (in the case of the study, an exercise test) had a 72 percent greater risk of stroke, compared to men with less reactive blood pressures. These men also had an 87 percent greater risk of ischemic stroke – those caused by blood clots rather than bursting of a brain vessel.[6]
Hypertension (Journal of the American Heart Association)

* Stress appears to increases atherosclerosis. Couples with no history of heart trouble who were hostile or domineering in their interactions were more likely to have tiny calcium deposits in coronary arteries, an early sign of arterial damage. The more anger and stress in their relationships, the more severe the atherosclerosis tended to be.[7]
Psychosomatic Medicine

* Common emotions such as tension, frustration, and sadness, trigger frequent and painless heart abnormalities that can lead to permanent heart damage. Study results show a direct, cause-and-effect relationship between negative emotions, an inadequate flow of blood to the heart, and increased risk of heart attack.[8]
Journal of the American Medical Association

* In response to stress, the adrenal glands release epinephrine, which in turn stimulates blood platelets (the cells responsible

for repairing blood vessels) to secrete ATP. In large amounts, ATP can trigger a heart attack or stroke by causing blood vessels to rapidly narrow, thus cutting off blood flow.[9]
New York Hospital, Cornell Medical Center

Immune system

* Stress appears to dramatically increase the ability of chemicals to pass through the blood-brain barrier, which normally protects the brain from toxins in the bloodstream. During the Gulf War, Israeli soldiers took a drug called pyridostigmine to protect themselves from chemical and biological weapons. Nearly 25 percent reported headaches, nausea, and dizziness – symptoms that occur only if the drug reaches the brain. In subsequent experiments with mice, researchers confirmed that those under stress had significantly greater permeability of chemicals through the blood-brain barrier than previous thought possible. Many of today's drugs are developed under the assumption that they will not enter the brain.[10]
Hebrew University, Jerusalem

* Being under high levels of stress for more than a month doubles a person's risk of a cold. Stress lasting more than two years nearly quadruples the risk. Being unemployed or underemployed, or having interpersonal difficulties with relatives or friends, has the greatest influence on risk.[11]
Carnegie Mellon University

* Stress has been found to lower immune function. Several studies of medical students at exam time showed significant drops in the numbers and activity of natural killer cells (key in fighting cancer cells and viruses), and a significantly lower percentage of T-helper cells in the blood (cells that arouse the immune response to fight off an infection).[12]
Psychosomatic Medicine, Journal of Behavioral Medicine, and Psychiatry Research

Aging

* Blood cells from women who had spent many years caring for a disabled child were, genetically, about a decade older than those from peers who had less caretaking responsibility. Severe emotional distress, like that caused by divorce, the loss of a job, or caring for an ill child or parent, appears to accelerate aging.[13]
Proceedings of the National Academy of Sciences

Arthritis

* In a study of 100 people with rheumatoid arthritis, levels of prolactin were twice as high among those reporting high degrees of interpersonal stress than among those not stressed. Prolactin migrates to joints where it initiates a cascade of events leading to swelling and pain.[14]
Arizona State University

Memory

* Stress can damage the brain's hippocampus, making it difficult to learn new things. Mice under stress continuously explored their surroundings, as if they had no ability to retain memory.[15]
University of South Florida

* Cortisol is produced by the body when under stress, and also increases with age, for reasons not yet known. People with high cortisol levels showed marked deficits in memory and a 14 percent decrease in the size of the hippocampus. Studies show that cortisol levels can be influenced by meditation and exercise, among other methods. Once they return to normal, memory ability returns we well.[16]
Nature Neuroscience

Mental health

* The percentage of Americans who report feeling close to having a serious nervous breakdown has increased from 17 percent of adults in 1957, when the survey was first conducted, to 26 percent in 2000.[17]
American Psychologist

Sleep

* Stress is one of the leading causes of insomnia. More than 50 percent of American adults have insomnia a few nights a week or more. 25 percent suffer from chronic insomnia (occurring most nights and lasting a month or longer). Twenty percent of adults experience daytime sleepiness severe enough to interfere with their daily activities a few days each week or more.[18]
National Sleep Foundation and Duke University Medical Center

Stress in the Workplace

Though it is difficult to quantify, researchers believe that stress is a significant cost to American business. The overall cost has been estimated at $300 billion a year,[19] including absenteeism, additional health costs incurred by those under stress, turnover, EAP costs, disability, and accidents. A small example: in a study of 44 hospitals, those that implemented a hospital-wide stress reduction training program experienced a 50 percent drop in medical errors and a 70 percent reduction in malpractice claims. The control group of twenty-two hospitals showed no change.[20]

Employee Perceptions of Stress

* The percent of full- or part-time workers reporting high job stress rose to 45 percent in 2002, from 37 percent in 2001 and

26 percent in 1999.[21]
Yankelovich Monitor, Annual Survey

* Thirty percent of adults report high job stress nearly every day. In one survey, more than a third of respondents were considering changing work because of job stress.[22]
Northwestern National Life Insurance

Economic impact

* The cost of stress to business has been estimated at:
    19% of absenteeism
    40% of turnover
    55% of EAP programs
    30% of short-term disability and long-term disability costs
    10% of drug-plan costs
    60% of the cost of workplace accidents[23]
What Stress Costs

* Individuals with stress and related disorders experience impaired physical and mental functioning, more workdays lost, increased impairment at work, and a high use of health care services. The disability caused by stress is comparable to disability caused by workplace accidents and common medical conditions such as hypertension, diabetes, and arthritis.[24]
Metabolism

* Health care expenditures are nearly 50 percent greater for workers who report high levels of stress.[25]
Journal of Occupational and Environmental Medicine

* Workers who must take time off work because of stress, anxiety, or a related disorder will be off the job for approximately 20 days.[26]
Bureau of Labor Statistics

Workplace stress and health

* Workers who spent most of their lives in a job in which they had little control (over things such as flexible hours and when to take a break) had a 43 percent increased risk of dying during their working life, as well as up to 10 years after they stopped working.[27]
Psychosomatic Medicine

* Ninety percent of physiological and psychological diseases among police officers and supervisors is attributable to prolonged work stress.[28]
FBI Law Enforcement Bulletin

* In a survey of real estate professionals, 62 percent of respondents routinely ended their workday with work-related neck pain. 44 percent reported fatigued eyes, 38 percent complained of hurting hands and 34 percent reported difficulty in sleeping. More than 50 percent of respondents said they often spend 12-hour days on work related duties and frequently skip lunch.[29]
American Demographics

* Unemployment tripled in Finland between 1991 and 1993. During this period and for seven years afterward, researchers followed municipal workers in four towns who survived the cutbacks. Those in work units with the most downsizing suffered twice the death rate from heart attack and stroke.[30]
British Medical Journal

* Air traffic controllers were found to have five times the incidence of hypertension compared to a control group in a less stressful occupation (second-class airmen).[31]
Journal of the American Medical Association

Meditation and health

Hundreds of studies have been conducted on meditation and its effects on the body. Significant benefits have been found for many health conditions, including heart disease, cholesterol, high blood pressure, insomnia, chronic pain, cancer, and immunity. Research on meditation has also shown significant improvements in mental health, memory, concentration, and productivity. Since 1992, new technology has allowed more accurate assessment of effects in the brain. Because meditation is a low-cost intervention with no side effects, it shows promise for relief of a wide range of societal and health problems.

Hospitalization

* In a study of health insurance statistics, meditators had 87 percent fewer hospitalizations for heart disease, 55 percent fewer for benign and malignant tumors, and 30 percent fewer for infectious diseases. The meditators consistently had more than 50 percent fewer doctor visits than did non-meditators.[32]
Psychosomatic Medicine

* Surgery patients who have learned simple relaxation and meditation techniques stay in the hospital an average of 1.5 days (12 percent) fewer than those in the control group. Results included faster recovery from surgery, fewer complications, and reduced postsurgical pains. This finding was consistent in 191 independent studies.[33]
University of Wisconsin, School of Nursing

Heart disease

* Patients recovering from heart attacks took a six-hour program of stress management training with mind/body techniques and emotional support. The result was a 50 percent reduction in subsequent rate of cardiac deaths.[34]

Psychosomatic Medicine

* Meditation lowers blood pressure in people who are normal to moderately hypertensive. This finding has been replicated by more than nineteen studies, some of which have shown systolic reductions among their subjects of 25 mmHg or more.[35]
The Physical and Psychological Effects of Meditation

* Stress management appears to be as beneficial as aerobic exercise in preventing major cardiac events. A group receiving standard care turned out to have the most cardiac events, such as heart attacks, open-heart surgery, and angioplasty. The group that studied stress management had fewer problems – equal to that of the aerobics group.[36]
American Journal of Cardiology

* Meditation may reduce atherosclerosis. In a study of 60 men and women over seven months, those practicing meditation showed a decrease of .098 millimeter in arterial wall thickness – an 11 percent decrease in the risk of heart attack, and a 7.7 to 15 percent reduction in the risk of stroke. The non-meditating control group showed an increase of .054 millimeter in wall thickness.[37]
Stroke, Journal of the American Heart Association

* Twenty-eight people with high levels of blocked arteries and high risk of heart attack were placed on a program with regular practice of meditation, yoga, a low-fat vegetarian diet, and exercise. Twenty people in the control group received conventional medical care endorsed by the AMA. At the end of a year, most of the experimental group reported that their chest pains had virtually disappeared; in 82 percent of the patients, arterial clogging had reversed. Those who were sickest at the start showed the most improvement. The control group had an increase in chest pain and arterial blockage worsened. (Follow-up

studies suggest that the stress-reduction element may be the most significant factor in achieving these results.)[38]
The Lancet

* Numerous studies have shown increases in circulation during meditation. Forearm blood flow increased in novice meditators by 30 percent. Frontal cerebral blood flow increased an average of 65 percent in experienced meditators, and remained elevated afterwards, with brief increases of up to 100–200 percent.[39]
The Physical and Psychological Effects of Meditation

* Patients with ischemic heart disease who practiced meditation for four weeks achieved significant reduction in the frequency of preventricular contractions. (Ischemic heart disease is decreased blood to the heart muscle that results in anginal chest pain and heart attacks.)[40]
The Lancet

* A group of patients who were trained in meditation and received angioplasty procedures showed significantly less anxiety, pain, and need for medication. In patients receiving heart surgery, the meditators had significantly lower incidence of postoperative rapid heart rate than the control group.[41]

Behavioral Medicine

* Three groups of heart patients were given usual care, exercise therapy, or stress management training. Patients in the exercise group and usual care group averaged 1.3 cardiac events by the fifth year of follow-up (bypass surgery, angioplasty, heart attack or death). Those in the stress management group averaged only 0.8 cardiac events.[42]
American Journal of Cardiology

Chronic pain

* Meditation and relaxation therapies are effective in treating chronic pain, and can markedly ease the pain of low back problems, arthritis, and headaches.[43]
National Institutes of Health (NIH)

* Those trained in meditation were able to reduce chronic pain by more than 50 percent. This gain was maintained even four years after the initial training.[44]
Clinical Journal of Pain

* Chronic pain patients attended a ten-session outpatient mind/body program including meditation training. They were able to reduce total monthly clinic visits for pain management by 36 percent during the subsequent year.[45]
The Clinical Journal of Pain

Insomnia

Seventy-five percent of long-term insomniacs who have been trained in relaxation, meditation, and simple lifestyle changes can fall asleep within 20 minutes of going to bed.[46]
Harvard Medical

* Behavioral and relaxation techniques are more effective than sleeping pills in treating chronic sleep-onset insomnia. In addition, sleeping pills lose their effectiveness as soon as they are discontinued.[47]
Archives of Internal Medicine

Cancer

* The progression of prostate cancer can be slowed or perhaps even reversed by changes in diet and lifestyle alone. Researchers studied 93 early-stage prostate cancer patients who had chosen

not to undergo conventional treatment but opted instead for a wait-and-see approach. The men were randomly placed into a lifestyle change group or a control group. The lifestyle patients were prescribed a vegan diet with fish oil and other supplements, moderate aerobic exercise, a daily one-hour period of relaxation via techniques such as yoga-based meditation and weekly participation in a support group. After a year, 6 of the control group underwent treatment because of disease progression, in contrast to none of the lifestyle patients. When serum from both groups was administered to prostate tumor lines, that of the improved lifestyle group inhibited tumor growth by 70 percent, compared to 9 percent in the control group. 232,000 U.S. men each year are diagnosed with prostate cancer, and 30,000 die of the condition.[48]
Journal of Urology

* Women who meditate and use guided imagery have higher levels of the immune cells known to combat tumors in the breast.[49]
Reported in Time Magazine, "The Science of Meditation"

Diabetes

* Meditation and relaxation may help diabetes. Those with type II diabetes who practiced meditation over six weeks showed significantly reduced blood sugar levels, compared to little or no change compared to the control group.[50]
Dissertation Abstracts International

Mental health

* A group of inner-city residents suffering from chronic pain, anxiety, depression, diabetes, and hypertension were trained in meditation. They experienced a 50 percent reduction in overall psychiatric symptoms, a 70 percent decrease in anxiety, and a

44 percent reduction in medical symptoms.[51]
Nurse Practitioner

* Meditation helped chronically depressed patients, reducing their relapse rate by half.[52]
Journal of Consulting and Clinical Psychology

* More than half of all patients who have had one or two episodes of clinical depression will relapse into another. The more episodes, the higher the risk. In a study of patients who had recovered from a depressive episode, 66 percent of those who learned meditation remained stable (no relapse) over a year, compared with 34 percent of the control group.[53]
University of Toronto

* A group of 90 cancer patients learned meditation. Compared to the non-meditating control group, those who had meditated for seven weeks reported a 65 percent reduction in moods (less depressed, anxious, angry, and confused) and a 31 percent reduction in symptoms of stress.[54]
Psychosomatic Medicine

* High blood lactate concentrations have been associated with anxiety and high blood pressure. Nine studies have reported significant declines of up to 33 percent in blood lactate during meditation, and a rate of decline nearly four times faster than the rate of decrease among people resting or in a premeditation period.[55]
The Physical and Psychological Effects of Meditation

Immune system and healing

* One of the treatments for psoriasis is ultraviolet light therapy, which patients report as being stressful. When patients

listened to meditation tapes during the ultraviolet light therapy, they healed approximately four times faster than the control group.[56]
Psychosomatic Medicine

* Medical students under stress during exam periods were taught meditation. The more they practiced, the higher the percentage of T-helper cells circulating in their blood (cells that arouse the immune response to fight off infection).[57]
Journal of Behavioral Medicine

* College students under stress at exam time showed decreases in salivary Immunoglobulin A (sIgA), a chemical that serves as the body's first line of defense against infection. Relaxation and meditation consistently lead to highly significant increases in sIgA concentrations.[58]
Journal of Psychosomatic Research

Women's health

* Women with severe PMS showed a 58 percent improvement in their symptoms after five months of daily meditation. Other studies showed overall improvements of 20–30 percent in symptoms in women with mild to severe PMS.[59]
Obstetrics and Gynecology

* Women struggling with infertility had less anxiety, depression, and fatigue following a 10-week meditation program, along with exercise and nutritional changes. Thirty-four percent became pregnant within six months.[60]
Fertility and Sterility

* Fifty-five mothers of infants in a neonatal intensive care unit were trained in relaxation and visualization. They produced twice as much milk as those receiving only routine care.[61]
Pediatrics

Aging

Meditation may enhance longevity and well-being. Relaxation techniques, creative word games, or meditation were taught to about 60 residents of nursing homes. In follow-up sessions, the meditators scored highest in improved learning ability, cheerfulness, and mental health, and lowest in blood pressure. Three years later, about one-third of the study group had died. All of the meditators, however, were still alive.[62]
Journal of Personality and Social Psychology

* Those who had been practicing meditation for more than five years were physiologically 12 years younger than their chronological age, as measured by reduction of blood pressure, and better near-point vision and auditory discrimination. Short-term meditators were physiologically 5 years younger than their chronological age. The study controlled for the effects of diet and exercise.[63]
International Journal of Neuroscience

* Brain scans of twenty people who meditated regularly showed increased thickness in regions of the cortex associated with higher functions like memory and decision making. Also, one area of the cortex seemed to have aged less quickly than in the non-meditators.[64]
Massachusetts General Hospital

* Meditation lowers blood cortisol levels. Older women who regularly practice meditation have a reduced cortisol response to stress. The longer a woman has been practicing, the less likely she is to react to stress with high levels of blood cortisol.[65]
New York Academy of Sciences

General health

* Meditation decreases oxygen consumption, heart rate, respiratory rate, and blood pressure, and increases the intensity of

alpha, theta, and delta brain waves – the opposite of the physiological changes that occur during the stress response.[66]
Harvard Medical School

* Thirty-five highly stressed individuals were trained to meditate. Over three months, they experienced a 46 percent
decrease in medical symptoms, compared with a slight increase in the control group.[67]
American Journal of Health Promotion

* Oxygen consumption is reduced during meditation, in some
studies by as much as 55 percent. Carbon dioxide elimination
is reduced by as much as 50 percent. Respiration rate is less-
ened, in some cases to one breath per minute, when twelve to
fourteen breaths per minute are normal.[68]
The Physical and Psychological Effects of Meditation

Productivity

* Twenty-five workers at Promega, a high tech company in
Wisconsin, reported feeling "stressed-out" and unhappy with
their jobs. Scans confirmed high levels of right-brain activity.
After eight weeks of meditation training and practice, the activity in the left side of their brains increased significantly. The
workers reported feeling happier, with a renewed sense of enthusiasm for their life and work. The control group showed no
change. At the end of the eight weeks, everyone received flu
shots to test immune responses. The meditators had more anti-
bodies against the flu virus than the non-meditators. Those
with the strongest immune response had the highest levels of
left-sided brain activity.[69]
University of Wisconsin

> Note: Brain scans show that meditation shifts activity in the
> prefrontal cortex (behind the forehead) from the right hemi-
> sphere to the left. People who have a negative disposition

tend to be right-prefrontal oriented; left-prefrontals have more enthusiasms, more interests, relax more, and tend to be happier.[70]

* Stress reduction has a significant impact on medical errors. Twenty-two hospitals that implemented a stress prevention program experienced a 50 percent drop in medical errors and a 70 percent reduction in malpractice claims. A control group of twenty-two hospitals that implemented no special stress reduction program showed no change in medical errors or malpractice claims.[71]
Journal of Applied Psychology [Also noted in Stress in the Workplace]

* Meditation increases concentration. Seventy-six Tibetan monks, all experienced meditators, were shown a different image in each eye. Normally, people's brains switch between the two images every 2.5 seconds. But the monks averaged about four seconds per eye, One monk was able to focus on one of the images for 723 seconds.[72]
Society for Neuroscience

* Meditation practices can lead to heightened cortical arousability plus decreased limbic arousability, so that perception is heightened and emotion is simultaneously reduced.[73]
The Physical and Psychological Effects of Meditation

* Researchers tested novice meditators on a button-pressing task requiring speed and concentration. Performance was greater at 40 minutes of meditation than after a 40-minute nap.[74]
The Boston Globe, November 23, 2005

* Managers and employees who regularly practiced meditation improved significantly in overall physical health, mental well-being, and vitality when compared to control subjects with similar jobs. Meditators reported significant reductions in health problems such as headaches and backaches, improved quality

of sleep, and a significant reduction in the use of hard liquor and cigarettes, compared to the control groups.[75]
Anxiety, Stress and Coping International Journal

* A study found significant improvements in relations with supervisors and co-workers after an average of eleven months practicing meditation, in comparison to the control group. Job performance and job satisfaction increased while desire to change jobs decreased.[76]
Academy of Management Journal

Addiction

* Meditation produced a larger reduction in tobacco, alcohol, and illicit drug use than either standard substance abuse treatments (including counseling, pharmacological treatments, relaxation training, and Twelve-Step programs) or prevention programs (such as programs to counteract peer pressure and promote personal development). Whereas the effects of conventional programs typically decrease sharply by three months, effects of meditation on total abstinence from tobacco, alcohol, and illicit drug ranged from 50 percent to 89 percent over an 18 to 22 month period of study.[77]
Alcoholism Treatment Quarterly

* Meditative self-awareness can reduce binge overeating. In a study of obese women, meditation training and awareness practice while eating (slowly savoring the flavor of a piece of cheese, being aware of how much is enough), reduced eating binges from an average of 4 per week to 1.5 per week.[78]
Journal of Health Psychology

* Ninety percent of those who practiced meditation twice each day had quit or decreased smoking by the end of the study, verses 71 percent for the once each day meditators, 55 percent

for those who were irregular or no longer practiced meditation, and 33 percent for the non-meditating group.[79]
Dissertation Abstracts International

* After three months of meditation, 50 to 75 percent of regular marijuana users decreased or stopped using marijuana, compared to 15 percent of the non-meditating control group. The longer people practiced meditation, the more likely they were to decrease or stop the use of marijuana.[80]
American Journal of Psychiatry

Children's health

* Forty-eight children who participated in a six-week meditation program showed significant improvements in behavior, self-esteem, and relationship quality. There was an average 35 percent improvement in ADHD symptoms. Of the 31 children taking medication for their ADHD, 11 were able to reduce their medications during the course of the program.[81]
Clinical Child Psychology and Psychiatry

* Middle school students who were exposed to relaxation and meditation techniques over a three year period scored higher on work habits, cooperation, and attendance and had significantly higher GPA's than non-meditating students.[82]
Journal of Research and Development in Education

REFERENCES

1 Herbert Benson, President, Harvard Mind Body Medical Institute.

2 C. Nowroozi, "How Stress Can Make You Sick." *Nation's Business*, 82 (12) (December, 1994): 82.

3 T. Chandola, "Chronic Stress at Work and the Metabolic Syndrome," *British Medical Journal* 332, (January, 2006): 521–525.

4 R. H. Rosenman, "The Questionable Roles of the Diet and Serum Cholesterol in the Incidence of Ischemic Heart Disease and Its 20th Century Changes," *Homeostasis* 34 (1993): 1–43.

5 W. F. Page and L. M. Brass, "Long-Term Heart Disease and Stroke Mortality Among Former American Prisoners of War of World War II and the Korean Conflict: Results of a 50-year Follow-Up," *Military Medicine* 166 (2001): 803–808.

6 S. A. Everson; G. A. Kaplan; D. E. Goldberg; J. T. Salonen, "Anticipatory Blood Pressure Response to Exercise Predicts Future High Blood Pressure in Middle-Aged Men," *Hypertension* 27 (1996): 1059–1064.

7 T. Smith, and L. C. Gallo, "Hostility and Cardiovascular Reactivity During Marital Interaction," *Psychosomatic Medicine* 61 (1999): 436–445.

8 E. C. D. Gullette, J. A. Blumenthal, et al, "Effects of Mental Stress on Myocardial Ischemia During Daily Life," *Journal of the American Medical Association* 277 (1997): 1521–1526.

9 T. Pickering, New York Hospital, Cornell Medical Center, reported in *Psychology Today*, (January 1996).

10 A. Friedman, D. Kaufer, J. Shemer, et al, "Pyridostigmine Brain Penetration Under Stress Enhances Neuronal Excitability and Induces Early Immediate Transcriptional Response," *Nature Medicine* 2(12) (1996): 1382–5.

11 S. Cohen, Carnegie Mellon University, reported in *Health Psychology*, (May, 1998).

12 *Psychosomatic Medicine* (1984), *Journal of Behavioral Medicine* (1986), and *Psychiatry Research* (1985).

13 E. Epel. E. Blackburn, et al, "Accelerated Telomere Shortening in Response to Life Stress," *Proceedings of the National Academy of Sciences* 101(49) (2004): 17312–17315.

14 K. Matt, Arizona State University, Reported in *Psychology Today* (January 1996).

15 D. Diamond, Tampa Veterans Affairs Hospital, University of South Florida, Experimental Biology Conference, Orlando (March, 2001).

16 S. J. Lupien, M. de Leon, S. de Santi, et al, "Cortisol Levels During Human Aging Predict Hippocampal Atrophy and Memory Deficits," *Nature Neuroscience* 1 (1998): 69–73.

17 *American Psychologist* (July, 2000).

18 National Sleep Foundation, 1999–2004 Surveys and M. Thakur, Duke University Medical Center.

19 American Institute of Stress, www.stress.org.

20 J. W. Jones, B. N. Barge, et al, "Stress and Medical Malpractice: Organizational Risk Assessment and Intervention," *Journal of Applied Psychology* 73(4) (1988): 727–735.

21 Yankelovich, Monitor Annual Survey of Consumer Attitudes and Lifestyles, 2002.

22 Northwestern National Life Insurance, "Employee Burnout: America's Newest Epidemic," Minneapolis, MN (1991).

23 Ravi Prakash Tangri, *What Stress Costs*, Oxford: Trafford Publishing, 2003.

24 M. Kalia, "Assessing the Economic Impact of Stress – the Modern Day Hidden Epidemic," *Metabolism* 51 (June, 2002): 49–53.

25 *Journal of Occupational and Environmental Medicine* (October, 1998).

26 Bureau of Labor Statistics, *http://stats.bls.gov/*, Tabular data, 1992–96: "Number and Percentage Distribution of Nonfatal Occupational Injuries and Illnesses Involving Days Away from Work,

by Nature of Injury or Illness and Number of Days Away From Work." Date accessed: 1998.

[27] B. Amick, "Relationship Between All-Cause Mortality and Cumulative Working Life Course Psychosocial and Physical Exposures in the United States Labor Market from 1968 to 1992," *Psychosomatic Medicine* 64 (May, 2002): 370–381.

[28] S. Standfest, "The Police Survivor and Stress," *The FBI Law Enforcement Bulletin* 65(5) (May, 1996): 7.

[29] G. Gallop-Goodman, "Unrest in the Cubicles: Workplace Stress," *American Demographics,* Integra Realty Survey (December 2000).

[30] J. Vahtera, and M. Kivimaki, "Organisational Downsizing, Sickness Absence, and Mortality: 10-Town Prospective Cohort Study," *British Medical Journal,* 328 (March 2004): 555–557.

[31] S. Cobb and R. Rose, "Hypertension, Peptic Ulcer, and Diabetes in Air Traffic Controllers," *Journal of the American Medical Association* 224, (1973): 489–92.

[32] D. Orme-Johnson, "Medical Care Utilization and the Transcendental Meditation Program," *Psychosomatic Medicine* 49 (1987): 493–507.

[33] E. Devine, "Effects of Psychoeducational Care for Adult Surgical Patients: A Meta-Analysis of 191 Studies," *Patient Education and Counseling* 19 (1992): 129–42.

[34] N. Frasure-Smith, "Long-Term Follow-Up of Ischemic Heart Disease Life Stress Monitoring Program," *Psychosomatic Medicine* 51 (September/October, 1989): 485–512.

[35] Michael Murphy and Steven Donovan, "The Physical and Psychological Effects of Meditation" (Institute of Noetic Sciences, 1997).

[36] J. Blumenthal, M. Babyak, J. Wei, et al, "Usefulness of Psychosocial Treatment of Mental Stress-Induced Myocardial Ischemia in Men," *American Journal of Cardiology* 89 (January 15, 2002): 164–168.

[37] A. Castillo-Richmond, et al, "Effects of Stress Reduction on Carotid Atherosclerosis in Hypertensive African Americans," *Stroke* 31(3) (March 2000): 568–73.

[38] D. Ornish, S. E. Brown, et al, "Can Lifestyle Changes Reverse Coronary Heart Disease," *The Lancet* 336 (July, 1990): 129–33.

[39] Riechert (1976); Wallace and Benson (1972); Jevning and Wilson (1978), "The Physical and Psychological Effects of Meditation" (1997).

40 H. Benson, S. Alexander, C. L. Feldman, "Decreased Premature Ventricular Contractions Through the Use of the Relaxation Response in Patients With Stable Ischemic Heart Disease," *The Lancet* (1975): ii:380–2.

41 J. Leserman, E. Stuart, M. Mamish, and H. Benson, "The Efficacy of the Relaxation Response in Preparing For Cardiac Surgery," *Behavioral Medicine*, (Fall, 1989): 111–17.

42 J. Blumenthal, M. Babyak, J. Wei, et al, "Usefulness of Psychosocial Treatment. . . .

43 NIH Technology Assessment Panel, "Integration of Behavioral and Relaxation Approaches Into the Treatment of Chronic Pain and Insomnia," *JAMA* 276(4) (1996): 313–8.

44 J. Kabat-Zinn, L. Lipworth, R. Burney, and W. Sellers, "Four Year Follow-Up of a Meditation-Based Program for the Self-Regulation of Chronic Pain," *Clinical Journal of Pain* 2 (1986): 159–173.

45 M. Caudill, R. Schnable, P. Zuttermeister, H. Benson, and R. Friedman, "Decreased Clinic Use by Chronic Pain Patients: Response to Behavioral Medicine Intervention," *The Clinical Journal of Pain* 7 (1991): 305–10.

46 Gregg Jacobs, Harvard Medical School, *Say Goodnight To Insomnia*, (New York: Owl Books, 1999).

47 G. D. Jacobs, E. F. Pace-Schott, R. Stickgold, M. Otto, "Cognitive-Behavioral Therapy and Pharmacotherapy For Insomnia," *Archives of Internal Medicine* 164 (September, 2004): 1888–1896.

48 D. Ornish, G. Weidner, W. R. Fair, et al, "Intensive Lifestyle Changes May Affect the Progression of Prostate Cancer," *Journal of Urology* 174(3) 2005: 1065–70.

49 Joel Stein, "The Science of Meditation" *Time Magazine* (August 2003).

50 H. Cerpa, "The Effects of Clinically Standardized Meditation on Type 2 diabetics," *Dissertation Abstracts International* 499 (1989): 3432.

51 B. Roth, T. Creaser, "Meditation-Based Stress Reduction: Experience With a Bilingual Inner-City Program," *Nurse Practitioner* 22(3) (1997): 150–2, 154, 157.

52 J. D. Teasdale, Z. V. Segal, J. M. G. Williams , V. Ridgeway, M. Lau, & J. Soulsby, "Reducing Risk of Recurrence of Major Depression Using Mindfulness-Based Cognitive Therapy," *Journal of Consulting and Clinical Psychology*, 68 (2000): 615–23.

[53] Zindal Segal, University of Toronto, reported in *Newsweek*, "The New Science of Mind and Body," (September 27, 2004).

[54] M. Speca, L. Carlson, E. Goodey, and M. Angen, "A randomized, Wait-List Controlled Clinical Trial: the Effect of a Mindfulness Meditation-Based Stress Reduction Program on Mood and Symptoms of Stress in Cancer Outpatients," *Psychosomatic Medicine* 62 (2000): 613–622.

[55] Michael Murphy and Steven Donovan, "The Physical and Psychological Effects of Meditation" (*Institute of Noetic Sciences*, 1997).

[56] J. Kabat-Zinn, E. Wheeler, T. Light, et al, "Influence of a Mindfulness-Based Stress Reduction Intervention on Rates of Skin Clearing in Patients With Moderate to Severe Psoriasis Undergoing Phototherapy (UVB) and Photochemotherapy *(PUVA),*" *Psychosomatic Medicine* 60 (1998): 625–632.

[57] J. Kiecolt-Glaser, R. Glaser, E. Strain, et al, "Modulation of Cellular Immunity in Medical Students," *Journal of Behavioral Medicine* 9 (1986): 311–20.

[58] M. R. Reid, et al, "The Effect of Stress Management on Symptoms of Upper Respiratory Tract Infection, Secretory Immunoglobulin A, and Mood in Young Adults," *Journal of Psychosomatic Research* 51(6) (December, 2001): 721–8.

[59] I. Goodale, A. Domar, and H. Benson, "Alleviation of Premenstrual Syndrome Symptoms With the Relaxation Response," *Obstetrics and Gynecology* 75(4) (1990): 649–55.

[60] A. Domar, M. Seibel, and H. Benson, "The Mind/Body Program for Infertility: a New Behavioral Treatment Approach for Women With Infertility," *Fertility and Sterility* 53(2) (1990): 246–49.

[61] D. K. Feher, L. R. Berger, D. Johnson, and J. B. Wilde, "Increasing Breast Milk Production for Preterm Infants With a Relaxation/Imagery Audiotape," *Pediatrics* 83 (1989): 57

[62] C. N. Alexander, E. J. Langer, et al, "Transcendental Meditation, Mindfulness, and Longevity: an Experimental Study With the Elderly," *Journal of Personality and Social Psychology* 57 (1989): 950–964.

[63] R. K. Wallace, M. C. Dillbeck, E. Jacobe, B. Harrington, "The Effects of the Transcendental Meditation on the Aging Process," *International Journal of Neuroscience* 16 (1982): 53–58.

[64] Massachusetts General Hospital, reported by Carey Goldberg, *The Boston Globe* (November 23, 2005).

[65] K. Walton, J. Fields, D. Levitsky, et al, "Lowering Cortisol and CVD Risk in Postmenopausal Women," *Annals of the New York Academy of Sciences* 1032 (December, 2004): 211–215.

[66] Herbert Benson, *The Relaxation Response,* (New York: HarperTorch, 1976).

[67] K. Williams, M. Kolar, B. Reger, & J. Pearson, "Evaluation of a Wellness-Based Mindfulness Stress Reduction Intervention: a Controlled Trial," *American Journal of Health Promotion* 15(6) (2001): 422–432.

[68] Michael Murphy and Steven Donovan, *"The Physical and Psychological Effects of Meditation"* (*Institute of Noetic Sciences,* 1997).

[69] R. Davidson, J. Kabat-Zinn, et al, "Alterations in Brain and Immune Function Produced by Mindfulness Meditation," *Psychosomatic Medicine* 65 (2003): 564–570.

[70] Ibid.

[71] J. W. Jones, B. N. Barge, B. D. Steffy, L. M. Fay, L. K. Kuntz, L. J. Wuebker, "Stress and Medical Malpractice: Organizational Risk Assessment and Intervention," *Journal of Applied Psychology* 73(4) (1988):727–735.

[72] O. Carter & J. Pettigrew, "Meditation Alters Perceptual Rivalry in Tibetan Buddhist Monks," *Society for Neuroscience* (2005), Abstract 583.12.

[73] Michael Murphy and Steven Donovan, "The Physical and Psychological Effects of Meditation" (*Institute of Noetic Sciences,* 1997).

[74] Reported in *The Boston Globe,* November 23, 2005.

[75] C. N. Alexander, G. C. Swanson, et al, "Effects of the Transcendental Meditation Program on Stress Reduction, Health, and Employee Development: A Prospective Study in Two Occupational Settings," *Anxiety, Stress and Coping: An International Journal* 6 (1993): 245–262.

[76] D. R. Frew, "Meditation and Productivity," *Academy of Management Journal,* 17 (1974), 362–368.

[77] C. N. Alexander, P. Robinson, M. Rainforth, "Treatment and Prevention of Drug Addiction," *Alcoholism Treatment* Quarterly 11 (1994): 11–84.